My Hand in His

Ancient Truths
in
Modern Parables

Herman W. Gockel

SAINT LOUIS

1 2 3 4 5 6 7 8 9 10   08 07 06 05 04 03 02 01 00 99

Contents

Preface

There are two statements in the gospel of Mark that, while they are separated by eight chapters, are nevertheless closely related. The first is written in the fourth chapter where we are told: "With many similar parables Jesus spoke the word to them, as much as they could understand. He did not say anything to them without using a parable" (verse 33). The second statement appears in the 12th chapter: "The large crowd listened to Him with delight" (verse 37).

There can be no doubt that for most of us, members of the large crowd that we are, there is something intriguing about a parable, especially the parables that have come to us from the lips of our Lord. In His parables, there is something that arrests our attention, holds our interest, and gives us a vivid insight into sacred truth, which, in many cases, could have come to us in no other way.

That is why the Savior repeatedly reduced the profound abstractions of His message to a simple narrative. He clothed His thoughts in flesh and blood and made them visual. To explain God's attitude toward His lost and straying children, for instance, Jesus told three short stories in quick succession: the stories of the lost sheep, the lost coin, and the lost son (Luke 15). Indeed, anyone who reads the four Gospels is bound to remember the Master Teacher and Master Evangelist as the Master Storyteller. "He did not say anything to them without using a parable. ... The large crowd listened to Him with delight."

It is this approach that I have sought to follow in these devotional readings. I make no claim to originality for all of the illustrations used. Many have been culled from my reading. For these I wish to give credit to their original authors. Others have been adapted or modified to suit my specific purpose. Others are original, based on personal observation or personal experience. All were originally published in the Christian magazine *This Day*.

It is my prayer that as readers journey through these pages they will gain fresh insights into the marvelous love of God as it has been revealed to us in Jesus Christ, His Son.

Herman W. Gockel

My Hand in His

A traveler in the Scottish Highlands saw a cluster of beautiful flowers far down the mountainside. He promised a reward to a shepherd boy if he would pick them. He even offered to let him down by a rope.

The boy eyed the stranger suspiciously, then without a word disappeared into the woods. In a moment he was back—with his father. He was willing to rappel down the mountainside provided the rope was in his father's hands.

Our Father in heaven permits our feet to travel along steep and slippery places, far down the mountainside of human suffering. But no matter how deep the valley or how difficult the descent, we always rest secure in the conviction that our times are in God's hands. He holds the rope!

We only travel as far down the hillside of adversity as His love would have us go. God knows our strength, and He knows our weakness. He knows even before we go down into the valley what flowers we will bring back with us—what lesson in humility, what lesson in trust, what lesson in Christian virtue. He will bring us up again as soon as we have gathered the flowers for which His love has sent us.

If ever there was a person who knew what it meant to descend from the mountaintop of prosperity and good fortune into the abyss of bitter disappointment, that person was David—the man "after God's own heart." Small wonder that David, on one occasion when he felt the ground crumbling beneath his feet, cast a pleading eye heavenward and exclaimed: "My times are in Your hands" (Psalm 31:15).

It has been the same with all believers of all time. It can be the same for you and me. Through faith in God's unchanging promises, especially through faith in the salvation promise fulfilled in His beloved Son, our hand is in the hand of God and we know that He will never let us go.

When the cross seems heaviest, when it seems that life has neither plan nor purpose, when it seems that I am pushed about by a blind and merciless fate, what comfort to remember that in every valley of affliction my hand is in His.

And with my hand in His, I am forever safe. His omnipotent hand will hold me. His affectionate hand will guide me. His merciful hand will forgive me.

> I am trusting You, Lord Jesus,
> Never let me fall.
> I am trusting You forever
> And for all.

He Loved Me!

Four-year-old Elizabeth sat in her accustomed church pew, closely snuggled against her mother's side. The organ was playing the prelude, and Elizabeth's eyes were fixed on the picture of Jesus on the front of her Sunday school lesson.

Finally, looking at her mother and pointing to the picture of the Savior, she whispered with a joy that lit up her features, "He loved me!"

Yes, Elizabeth, He loved you! If only we who are older could always remember with joy and gratitude the love that He had in His heart for all of us! If only we could repeat, with the same fervency and the same affection, those simple words of the apostle Paul: "[He] loved me and gave Himself for me" (Galatians 2:20).

All that we need to know for time and for eternity is summed up in the simple sweetness of those tender words. Does the world hate me? He loved me! Do I find the way hard, the path dark, the night lonely, the world friendless? He loved me! Does the shadow of tomorrow's burden haunt my every step and cause my feet to falter? He loved me—and His love can never change. His love is everlasting.

Or do my sins seek to cause my heart alarm? My crimson record? My restless conscience? I need not fear: "Jesus gave Himself for me!" He took my sins to Calvary's cross and drowned them in the depths of His unending love. He bore my guilt. He paid my debt. He endured my punishment. He suffered all—He gave Himself for me!

What a blessed, soul-reviving thought to inscribe across the threshold of each new day! Tomorrow morning, every morning, every hour of the day and every day of the week, our hearts can be filled with the glad assurance: My Savior loves me! He gave Himself for me!

Just as Elizabeth looked into the face of her mother, we can lift grateful hearts heavenward and exclaim:

> Oh, the height of Jesus' love,
> Higher than the heav'ns above,
> Deeper than the depths of sea,
> Lasting as eternity!

Love that found me—wondrous
   thought—
Found me when I sought Him not.

The Sense of Sin

A Christian woman came to her pastor with a perplexing problem. She had been regular in her church attendance, conscientious in her daily prayers, and consistent in her attendance at the Lord's Supper. However, she had been unable to rid herself of a haunting sense of sin.

"Why is it," she asked, "that my girlfriends who never go to church, and who freely admit that they have never taken religion seriously, are never troubled by any consciousness of guilt?"

Her problem was not new to the pastor. "Tell me," he said, "if I were to lay a hundred pounds of steel on a corpse, would it feel the load?"

"No. I'm sure it wouldn't," the woman replied.

"Why not?" he asked.

"Because the corpse has no life in it and is unable to feel the weight," she answered.

"Exactly!" replied the pastor. "And that is

15

why the person who is still indifferent to spiritual needs can say that she doesn't feel the weight of sin. She's dead—spiritually."

It always has been true that the Christian is more conscious of personal unworthiness—in the sight of God than the careless unbeliever. David admitted: "I know my transgressions, and my sin is always before me" (Psalm 51:3). The apostle Paul, whom God used mightily to spread the Gospel, lamented: "I know that nothing good lives in me .... What a wretched man I am!" (Romans 7:18, 24).

There really is nothing surprising in the Christian's consciousness of sin. People who walk in darkness are unconscious of smudges on their bodies; but if they walk into the light, they immediately become conscious of their dirty hands.

Christians walk in light. And the closer we walk to the Light of Life, the more conscious we become of our soiled garments. Nor is there anything surprising in our sensitivity to personal guilt. We have seen our sin in terms of Calvary. It was a sensitive heart, a Christian heart, that wrote:

You who think of sin but lightly
Nor suppose the evil great
Here may view its nature rightly,
Here its guilt may estimate.

No, there was nothing at all surprising in the woman's concern over her personal sin. In fact, her deep concern was a sign that the Spirit of God was working in her heart. Yet she had no reason to worry. For the same Bible that told her that she was a sinner in God's sight also tells her: "Whenever our hearts condemn us ... God is greater than our hearts, and He knows everything" (1 John 3:20).

God, who is greater than our hearts, looks at us not in our sins, but in Christ. In Christ there is abundant pardon and mercy. As the apostle Paul assures us: "Therefore, there is now no condemnation for those who are in Christ Jesus" (Romans 8:1).

Sinners? Yes. But forgiven sinners. Forgiven through Christ.

The Secret of the Open Door

It happened many years ago on a cool October morning in a seaside village in England. A pastor was visiting in a cobbler's shop. He watched the cobbler pound the leather with his hammer and listened as the happy cobbler hummed a merry tune.

Looking around the dingy little shop with its cramped quarters and its crowded shelves, the pastor marveled that the man didn't seem depressed.

Finally, the pastor asked, "Don't you ever get tired of this narrow life—the same thing day after day in this crowded little room?"

The cobbler walked to a back door, opened it wide, and said, "When I start feeling depressed, Pastor, I just open this door."

As the door swung open, the room was flooded with a new glory. Within the twinkling of an eye, the cramped little shop had been transformed by the vastness of its new relationship to the fields and skies and rolling sea—and to the God who created all of it.

It is much the same with life in general. We are all in danger of living locked inside the closet of our immediate circumstances, looking at the same dark walls day after day—the walls of our gloomy thoughts, walls which we have placarded with our own insurmountable problems.

How different when we open the door and see how God has linked our lives to His eternal purposes, to the whole panorama of His love and beauty as revealed in Jesus Christ, our Savior! How different when the fresh air and sunlight of eternity flood into the dark and dingy cubicles of time!

Do our problems look too big for us? Are the walls of life closing in on us, crushing out all faith and joy and hope? Open the door! Look out! Look up! Look into the vastness of God's love as He Himself reveals it!

On the far horizon, we see those words of immeasurable assurance: "If God is for us, who can be against us? He who did not spare His own Son, but gave Him up for us all—how will He not also, along with Him, graciously give us all things?" (Romans 8:31–32). "All things" includes the inner joy our heart seeks.

"Love That Found Me"

In the timber mountains of the Northwest, a 5-year-old was lost. Night came. The citizens and rangers searched frantically in every cave and on every mountainside. Snow began to fall. Flake upon flake created a blanket of gleaming white that covered the floor of the forest, but Bobby could not be found.

The next morning, the weary father, fatigued from the all-night search, kicked against what seemed to be a log in his path. When the snow fell away, a small boy stretched, yawned, sat up, and exclaimed: "Oh, Daddy! I've found you at last!"

Now—who found whom?

In his excitement, Bobby might say: "Oh, Daddy, I've found you at last!" The bleeding heart of the older man knew that it was he—not Bobby—who had done the searching and the finding.

We sometimes talk about "finding" God. We may speak of the quest for God, the search for certainty, and the discovery of the divine. But God did not get lost—we did! Nor did we find God—God found us. In that precious "lost and found" chapter of St. Luke's gospel (chapter 15), it was the sheep that was lost, not the shepherd; the coin that was lost, not the woman; and it was the prodigal son, not the prodigal father.

If we are members of Christ's church, it is not because of any decision we made. The decision was God's. He found us. He found us outside, and He brought us inside.

If anyone had a right to say that he had "found God," surely Martin Luther might have said so. But what did he say? "I believe that I cannot by my own reason or strength believe in Jesus Christ, my Lord, or come to Him. But the Holy Ghost has called me by the Gospel." Luther did not find God. God found Luther and by the power of His Spirit, working through His Word, made Martin Luther an heir of heaven.

As we contemplate the wonders of God's love as revealed in the Bible, we thank Him for bringing us into the warmth and light of faith. We are in the Shepherd's keeping because God, from eternity, saw us out in the darkness of sin and decreed that we should be brought into the shelter of His fold.

The entire distance between God and us was covered by God. We are no longer lost because God found us! "This is love," writes John, "not that we loved God, but that He loved us" (1 John 4:10). That was the marvelous thought that prompted the poet to exclaim:

> Love that found me—wondrous
>   thought—
> Found me when I sought Him not.

Just a Day at a Time

Thoughts at the Turn of the Year

An anxious patient, lying on her sickbed, asked her doctor, "How long will I have to lie here and suffer?"

"Just a day at a time," replied the physician.

Just a day at a time! What a wonderful philosophy of life—especially as we turn the pages of our crisp new calendars and scan the 365 empty boxes into each of which, God willing, we will pour 24 hours of living.

Just a day at a time the new year will come to us with its new challenges, its new tasks, its new hopes, and its new fears. Thank God that we do not have to live the entire new year at once! It comes only a day at a time. Even tomorrow is never ours until it becomes today.

It is a blessed secret to be able to live just a day at a time. Those who have seen the crushing burden of sin lifted by Calvary's cross can carry their little burdens, however heavy, until nightfall. Those who know that their Savior has completed the tremendous work of redemption can perform their own tasks, however hard, just for a day. Those who have seen the patience of their Lord and Savior can live patiently, lovingly, helpfully, until the sun goes down.

God gives us night to shut down the curtain of darkness on our little days. We cannot see beyond, nor do we need to. Tomorrow is in God's hands—He is asking us only to live today.

So as we stand on the threshold of a brand-new year—a year that will record great changes in the history of our world, in the history of our families, and in our personal history. But we don't need to be frightened by the overwhelming possibilities. Instead, we can find comfort and strength in the fact that God has cut the coming year into smaller pieces, and we will live it just a day at a time.

God has promised us that our strength will equal our days (Deuteronomy 33:25). We have God's assurance that each day throughout the coming year, even each day throughout all the coming years, will find us equipped with the strength necessary to meet the challenges and more than overcome.

We don't need to live February in January. We don't need to live tomorrow today. Above all, we don't need to fear the prospect of an unknown future. Our all-wise, almighty, eternal God—in whom there are no yesterdays and no tomorrows—has gone ahead. When we reach our own tomorrow, we will find Him there.

Lord, for tomorrow and its needs
I do not pray.
Keep me, my God, from stain of sin
Just for today.

Let me both diligently work
And duly pray.
Let me be kind in word and deed
Just for today.

Let me in season, Lord, be brave,
In season gay.
Let me be faithful to Your grace
Just for today.

"Shut Out" and "Shut In"

Lenten Thoughts

Mr. Brown had just stepped from a crowded store into a telephone booth. He needed to call home. But try as hard as he would, he could not distinguish the voice at the other end of the line—and the message was lost in the clatter and clamor of the crowded store.

Finally, he managed to catch one sentence: "John, dear" said the voice, "please close the door." He had forgotten to close the door to the booth, and the noises of the store had drowned out the distant voice from home.

As we step from the busy, noisy world into the hush and quiet of the Lenten season, we have every reason to make sure that we have closed the doors behind us. We dare not run the risk of missing the "still, small voice" that speaks to the Christian heart through the contemplation of the suffering Savior.

There are some things that we will have to shut out, and there are some things that we will have to shut in, if we wish to make this season a period of spiritual refreshment.

Ours is a busy, noisy world, which does not describe only the throbbing world of manufacture, trade, and commerce. It describes the busy world that has broken into the midst of the family circle: 12-year-old Mark with basketball practice and homework; 18-year-old Ellen with college plans, a part-time job, and social obligations; dad with his evening meetings and household tasks; mom with her full-time job and household responsibilities; the television set with its daily fare of entertainment and excitement—all this combines to resemble the noisy store against which Mr. Brown had forgotten to shut the door.

We have to face the facts: If we are to hear the "still, small voice" within our family circle during this Lenten season, we have to shut out some things that have assumed places of importance in our daily living.

We also have to shut some things in. Have you grown remiss in your personal, private prayers? Ask the Holy Spirit to help you find time during the coming weeks to shut yourself in with God for daily spiritual communion. Have you permitted family worship to be crowded out of your regular routine? Have you passed on daily study of God's Word because other interests have entered the picture? Return to the Word and ask the Spirit to bless your time of reading and reflection.

There is a message in the Lenten season, a message from the Father's heart to ours. It is a message of peace and pardon, of courage and strength, of life and hope. It comes to us through the wounds and death of Jesus Christ, our Savior.

During this Lenten season, ask yourself: Have I closed the doors against the intrusions of a busy world that would rob me of that message?

Easter Triumph

During the battle of Waterloo, the people of England depended on a system of semaphore signals to learn about the tide of battle. One of these signals was located on the tower of Winchester Cathedral.

Late in the day, it flashed the news: "Wellington defeated!" At that moment a sudden English fog obscured the signal. News of the disaster spread throughout the city. The whole countryside was steeped in dark despair. Suddenly the fog lifted, and the remainder of the message could be read. Instead of only two words being flashed, there were four. The complete message read: "Wellington defeated the enemy!" In a moment, sorrow turned to joy, defeat to victory.

So it was when Jesus was laid in the tomb on that first Good Friday. Hope had died, even in the hearts of Christ's most loyal friends. After the frightful crucifixion, the fog of disappointment and disillusionment had settled on the faithful few. They had read only part of the divine message. "Christ defeated!" was all they knew.

On the third day the impenetrable fog of despair lifted. The completed message flashed to the world. The message was not about defeat, but about victory; not about death, but about life. The completed Easter message was a triumphant shout: Christ defeated death!

Good Friday and Easter are inseparable in God's great plan of redemption. St. Paul wrote to the Christians in Rome that Christ "was delivered over to death for our sins and was raised to life for our justification" (Romans 4:25).

On Good Friday the Savior was offered up as the atoning sacrifice for the sins of all people ("delivered over to death for our sins"). But on Easter morning, the heavenly Father raised His Son to proclaim to all people everywhere that He had accepted the payment for the world's iniquity ("raised to life for our justification").

Easter, therefore, is preeminently a day of triumph. It is the day on which the Son of God emerged victorious over sin, death, hell, and the grave.

He lives triumphant from the grave;
He lives eternally to save;
He lives exalted, throned above;
He lives to rule His Church in love.

He lives, all glory to His name!
He lives, my Savior, still the same;
What joy this blest assurance gives:
I know that my Redeemer lives!

Greater Than Our Hearts

There are moments in our lives when we look into the secret chambers of our hearts for evidence that we are God's children—and we fail to find that evidence! Searching our souls for assurance of salvation, we find assurance only of our sin. Our heart condemns us, accuses us of innumerable transgressions, and finally confronts us with the crushing judgment: You are not a Christian!

It is at moments such as these that the divine assurance of a memorable statement of St. John falls like sweetest music on our soul. "Whenever our hearts condemn us," he writes, "God is greater than our hearts, and He knows everything" (1 John 3:20). Though our hearts condemn us a thousand times, though its inner precincts roar and shout endless accusations, "God is greater than our hearts, and He knows everything."

To anyone but a Christian, it is a terrible

thought to realize that God "knows everything." Among those things that must be part of His knowledge are the unnumbered sins that lurk within our hearts like skeletons in a closet. The unforgiven sinner seeks desperately to hide them from the all-seeing eye of an all-knowing God.

For the Christian there is comfort in the fact that God "knows everything." Why? What does God know that can reverse the terrible judgment of our hearts? What does God know that our deceitful hearts have failed to tell us?

Right there is the difference between the Christian faith and all the religions that humans have devised. God looks at us through Christ! He certainly knows that we are sinners, but He also knows that in Christ our guilt has been atoned, in Christ our sins have been washed away. He knows that in Christ our sin-stained lives have been accounted righteous in His sight.

God knows these things, and there is never a moment when He does not know them. Our hearts may forget—but God knows. Just as a heavy storm cloud may blot out the sun for a moment but can never remove the sun from the skies, so our little moments of doubt and despair can never erase the sun of God's mercy from the firmament of His promises.

Our hearts, forgetful of God's mercy, may confront us with the claims of God's consuming justice. But ever mindful of His Son's atonement, God confronts us with the sweet assurance: "Take heart, My son, My daughter; your sins are forgiven" (Matthew 9:2 paraphrased).

Therefore, let heart, soul, mind, or whatever else tell me that I am lost. It doesn't matter! My source of assurance rests in God's all-knowing love. The anchor of my soul has found its hold in the eternal Rock of Ages. He is "greater than my heart." He knows all things. And *He* tells me that I am saved.

The Beauty Is Inside

It was a hot summer day. Two high school girls had spent most of their Sunday afternoon in a leisurely stroll through the downtown section of the city. They found themselves directly in front of a huge cathedral. Looking at the lofty stained-glass window, which their art teacher had told them to be sure to see, one of the girls said: "Nothing beautiful in there! Just a lot of dirty glass."

An older woman, overhearing the remark, walked up to the girls and said, "You can't judge the beauty of a stained-glass window from the outside. Why don't you step inside?"

The girls went inside, and before they knew it, they were standing motionless and enthralled, their faces bathed in a symphony of color that was pouring from the stained-glass window. The woman was right: You can't judge a stained-glass window from the outside.

The same is true of the Bible. If you really

want to know if the Bible is God's Word, there is only one way to find out: Go inside. All the fine arguments, all the logical proofs, all the compelling evidence based on historical study will not mean as much as a reverent reading of the book itself.

The strongest evidence that the Bible has been given to us by God is evidence that cannot be passed from one person to another. It is a conviction that the Holy Spirit pours into the hearts of those who "go inside"—of those who read the book.

There is, of course, other evidence of the Bible's divine authorship. In more than 2,000 instances, the Bible identifies itself as the Word of God. Again and again its prophecies have been fulfilled. Jesus Himself placed His stamp of divine approval on the Scriptures. Wherever the Bible has gone, it has left a trail of blessing. Nowhere else in all the world could people have found such a way of escape from sin and hell as God has given them in one simple Bible verse: John 3:16.

These are all valid ways of "proving" that the Bible is God's Word. But like the young girls in the story above, it is possible to discuss all these "proofs" while standing on the outside of the Book and miss the greatest proof of all: the witness of the Holy Spirit through the power of the Word itself.

The apostle Peter tells us that we are born again not through arguments about the Bible, but "through the living and enduring word of God. … And this is the word that was preached to you" (1 Peter 1:23, 25).

The best advice to the honest inquirer about the Bible is: Go inside. That is where its beauty lies.

In the Upper Branches

An elderly woman had been confined to her bedroom for several years. Each spring she watched from her window as the same robin returned and built its nest high in a nearby tree.

One morning she called her daughter to her room and said nervously, "Look! Our robin is building her nest in one of the lower branches this year. I'm afraid the neighbor's cat can reach it."

A few days later, the woman looked out of her window to find the ground beneath the branch covered with feathers. The neighbor's cat had indeed found the lower branch within its reach—and the robin was dead!

As Christians we, too, have the choice of building our lives in the "upper branches" or in the "lower." We have the choice of living thrillingly close to God or dangerously close to the world. We have the choice of filling our minds with thoughts of goodness, love, and lofty aspiration or filling our minds with the mean and the low and the trivial.

We are living in the lower branches, for instance, when we cultivate a taste for books and magazines that pander to the lower passions; when we frequent places of amusement that cater to the lusts of the flesh; when we associate with companions we know delight in flouting purity and decency. How many people have built their lives in these lower branches and been snatched, almost unaware, by the Tempter and hurled to destruction.

We reside in the upper branches, removed farther from the Tempter's wiles, when we spend time daily with our Savior; when we occupy ourselves with His work; when we take an active part in worship and church activities; when we dine at the Lord's Table; when we associate with Christian friends; and when we fill our minds with those thoughts we can lay in the presence of the Master.

That is what the apostle Paul had in mind when he wrote: "Whatever is true, whatever is noble, whatever is right, whatever is pure, whatever is lovely, whatever is admirable—if anything is excellent or praiseworthy—think about such things" (Philippians 4:8). People who fill their minds with "such things" live in the upper branches, and the crafty enemy of their souls will not find them to be easy prey. Of those who have "set [their] minds on things above," the apostle says their life "is now hidden with Christ in God" (Colossians 3:3).

Scripture admonishes us to "live by the Spirit," that is, to live on the level of the things of God. Then it adds the promise: "and you will not gratify the desires of the sinful nature" (Galatians 5:16). Have you built your nest in the upper or in the lower branches?

When Disappointment Comes

At the Botanical Gardens at Oxford, England, a fine pomegranate was cut down almost to the root because it bore nothing but leaves. Sometime later the keeper was able to report that a marvelous transformation had taken place and the tree was now bearing fruit in abundance. All that had been needed was to cut back the tree—and to cut back the tree severely.

Our heavenly Father sometimes finds it necessary to "cut back" the trees that are growing in His garden. We Christians are those trees—planted, cultivated, and nurtured by the miracle of His grace. The Bible says of us: "Every branch that does bear fruit He prunes so that it will be even more fruitful" (John 15:2). Notice! This pruning is done on the branches that are bearing fruit—so they will bring forth more fruit. The brittle brush and useless twigs must be cut away to assure and to multiply the yield.

Sometimes we wonder why devout and pious Christians, men and women who strive to conform their lives to the will of Christ, suffer one disappointment after another. Why do the righteous suffer bitter visitations at the hands of a merciful Father?

The complete answer to that question will never be given this side of heaven. But God has revealed just enough of His design for us to pin our faith to. "Every branch that does bear fruit He prunes so that it may will be even more fruitful." We will be better, more fruitful, because of the cut back.

If ever someone underwent frequent prunings, it was the apostle Paul. In 2 Corinthians 11:24–33, he opens his life like a book and displays the countless scars of the pruning hook of God's unsearchable providence. He was beaten with rods, stoned, shipwrecked, hungry, thirsty, cold, and naked. Yet no one will deny that the life of this man of God was more fruitful because of these painful visitations.

So it is with everyone whom God has made His own through faith in Christ. Has our heavenly Father perhaps found it necessary to cut back drastically some branch in our life on which we had pinned our hopes? Have we experienced such a cut back through the loss of health? the loss of wealth? the loss of a beloved family member? Have we had to taste the bitter ashes of disillusionment?

These are painful "cut backs," but they are "cut backs" with a gracious purpose. We can remember that when the days of pruning come, God is not cutting down the tree—He is improving it.

Remember
Whose Child You Are

The story is told of a boy who was leaving home for college. His father had included him in the morning prayer at the breakfast table, asking God to protect him and to grant him success in the education that he was undertaking.

Rising from the table, the young man expected to receive some final bit of advice and instruction from his father. He was surprised when, after a moment's silence, the older man merely placed his hand on his shoulder, looked at him fondly, and said: "Remember whose son you are!"

Should the father have said more than that?

We are children temporarily away from our Father's house. "How great is the love the Father has lavished on us, that we should be called children of God!" exclaims the apostle John (1 John 3:1). Yes, we are sons and daughters of God through Christ!

In our heavenly Father's letters to us, the Holy Scriptures, He has often admonished us to remember whose children we are. "You were once darkness," God writes to the Ephesians and to us through the apostle Paul, "but now you are light in the Lord. Live as children of light" (Ephesians 5:8). The Savior Himself has told us: "Let your light shine before men, that they may see your good deeds and praise your Father in heaven" (Matthew 5:16).

How have we been behaving away from home, away from our Father's house? Have we been reflecting positively on our family name—"children of God"?

As a rule, we are extremely careful to protect the good name of our earthly family. The Smith children are eager to protect the good name of the Smith parents and the Smith parents are eager to protect the good name of the Smith children. A deep sense of family loyalty and pride makes everyone want to do only those things that reflect positively on the name of Smith. As we daily remember—in our home, at our job, and while we play—that we are the "children of God," we will seek to reflect positively on the name of Him whom we call "Father."

As the children of God by faith in Christ, it is inevitable that we share some of the family traits common to all God's children: love, mercy, forbearance, righteousness, honesty, faithfulness. Just as the children of earthly parents frequently take after one or both parents, so those who have come to faith in Christ Jesus take after their Father and Brother. Daily, through the power of the Holy Spirit, we become more like Christ—more loving, more patient, more kind, more honest, more truthful, more righteous.

Yes, it's a good thing to remember whose children we are!

Give God Your Life

The evangelist Dwight Moody was conducting services in a town in England. Upon returning to his friend's home in the evening, the friend inquired: "Well, how many were converted tonight?"

"Two and a half," Moody replied.

"What do you mean?" asked the friend. "Was it two adults and a child?"

"No," replied the evangelist. "It was two children and an adult. The children have given their lives to Christ in their youth while the adult has come with only the fraction of his life that is left."

While it is true that the angels of heaven rejoice over "every sinner that repents," no matter how young or how old, it is also true that the person who comes to faith in later years gives the Lord a proportionately smaller fraction of this earthly life.

How much of our life are we giving to

the Lord? The question is not how much of our time, how much of our talents, or how much of our money have we placed at His disposal. It is how much of our life. We read that before the Macedonians gave anything to the Lord, they "gave themselves first to the Lord" (2 Corinthians 8:5).

Have we surrendered ourselves to the Lord in that way? It's a comparatively simple matter to pry ourselves loose from a $5 bill or from an evening's entertainment and to give the money or the evening to the Lord. It's an entirely different matter to pry ourselves loose from our self and to put our life wholly at God's disposal.

Yet that is what the Lord expects of us and nothing less. Out of gratitude for His surpassing mercy, revealed to us and to all people on Calvary's cross, our will is replaced by His. Our lives are surrendered to God. We say with Paul: "I have been crucified with Christ and I no longer live, but Christ lives in me. The life I live in the body, I live by faith in the Son of God, who loved me and gave Himself for me" (Galatians 2:20).

Can we honestly say that? Can we honestly say that the life we now live is being lived "by faith in the Son of God, who loved me and gave Himself for me"? Can we honestly say, "I no longer live, but Christ lives in me"? If not, we may have given God some of our money, some of our time, some of our talents, but we have not given Him our life.

Take my life, O Lord, renew,
Consecrate my heart to You.

The Clocks of Heaven

Travelers to distant countries have been known to keep one timepiece set to the time of their native land so—for reasons of sentiment—they might always know what time it is back home.

In a similar sense, the Christian pilgrim matches one clock, the clock of faith and trust, to the clocks in the Father's house above. There is a measurement of time that is known only to the believing and trusting heart—a measurement that is divided not into days and hours and minutes, but into the constantly repeated assurances of God's eternal promises.

The answer to a prayer, the lifting of a cross, the deliverance from a long-felt sorrow, or the granting of a long-sought pleasure are all scheduled for fulfillment not according to earthly clocks and calendars, but according to the clocks of eternity hanging on the walls of our Father's house.

God never comes too late with too little or too soon with too much. He is always on time—His time. His delays, when delays occur, are always the delays of love. His "little whiles" (John 16:19) are always preludes to greater revelations of His mercy.

For Joseph, thrown into the pit by his jealous brothers or later cast into prison by an angry Potiphar, it may have seemed that the clocks of heaven had stopped. It may have seemed that the promises of God were empty, vain, and futile. But Joseph lived to see the day when all the clocks of heaven struck the hour of God's fulfillment (Genesis 50:20).

Our heavenly Father assures us: "For a brief moment I abandoned you, but with deep compassion I will bring you back" (Isaiah 54:7). Again He says: "Weeping may remain for a night, but rejoicing comes in the morning" (Psalm 30:5).

What comfort to know that because of the life, death, and resurrection of our beloved Savior, all the clocks of heaven have been set for our eternal welfare! With David, we can say in all confidence: "My times are in Your hands" (Psalm 31:15) because we know that our times are in the hands of Him who loved us and gave Himself for us.

It is true that there are times when it seems that the clocks of heaven run slowly. There are times when the purposes of God seem "past finding out," but in Christ we know that they are always the purposes of love.

Ashamed of Being a Christian

The story is told of a Christian young man who spent several months in a Canadian lumber camp. The camp was notorious for its rough and lawless characters.

When the young man returned to his home a few months later, one of his friends asked how he had fared in that kind of company.

"Oh, fine," the man replied. "They never caught on that I was different!"

Several months in the company of godless people and they never "caught on" that he was a Christian! What a perfect record of shameful denial! In the company of unbelievers, this man had been afraid to admit that he was a Christian because he wasn't ready to bear the consequences.

Before we censure this man too strongly, or before we begin to congratulate ourselves in self-righteous satisfaction, ask yourself: What is my record in the company of Christ's enemies?

Has it really been much better? How have I hidden my colors, dodged the issues, shaved the truth, trimmed the sails? What flagrant, base denial of the Savior will my record reveal?

We read this about John the Baptist: "He did not fail to confess, but confessed freely" (John 1:20). All too often we do "fail to confess."

Perhaps these scenarios sound familiar: The Christian student who for the first time finds himself associating with the "in crowd." The Christian college student who finds herself with companions who flout decency and purity. The Christian businessperson who finds himself in the midst of blatant scoffers. How often do we find the strength and courage to stand up for Christ and to demonstrate our loyalty to Him?

In reality, we often manage to hide our colors—uncomfortably perhaps, but successfully—and later breathe a sigh of relief if our godless companions never "caught on" that we belong to Christ. There are glorious exceptions, but why should the precious name of Christ be denied so often?

Surely, each of us has reason to ask God to forgive our sins of cowardice. Then, like Simon Peter after he had been forgiven and restored

by the Lord whom he had shamefully denied,
we can pray for courage to confess our Savior
before friend and foe alike.

> Ashamed of Jesus, that dear friend
> On whom my hopes of heav'n depend?
> No; When I blush, be this my shame,
> That I no more revere His name.

The Fire on the Altar

A group of engineers working for the Tennessee Valley Authority came to the humble cottage of an elderly man. The engineers wanted to persuade the man to vacate the property to make way for their engineering project.

The old man was kind but firm. He had made up his mind to stay in the home where his father and grandfather had lived. The engineers told the man they would build him a new house to replace the dilapidated shack to which he had become attached.

"You don't understand," the old man insisted. "When my father was ready to leave this world, he called me to his bedside and told me that this house had been built by his forefathers and that the fire started in this fireplace had never been permitted to go out. My father made me promise, before he died, that I would never let this fire go out. I could never think of going back on my word."

Only after the engineers assured the man that they would build him a new house and carry some of the fire from the old fireplace to the new one did the man consent to leave his property.

If only we were as eager to keep the altar fires burning in our hearts and in our homes as this gentleman was to keep the fire burning in that fireplace!

The flame of Christian faith, of love, and devotion that burned brightly when you first came to faith—is it still burning as brightly in your hearts and lives today? The fire on the family altar, the daily habit of family devotions and prayer, the daily study of the family Bible, the daily expression of a common family faith—is that fire still burning brightly? Or has the fire long since flickered, sputtered, and finally succumbed to the winds of indifference, preoccupation, doubt, and disbelief? Alas, many a fire on the altar has been permitted to languish and die.

The fire on the altars of our hearts and homes is rekindled every day as we remember and celebrate our Baptism. Ask God for a living family faith—a faith in Jesus Christ as Savior and as family Friend.

Oh, blest that house; it prospers well!
In peace and joy the parents dwell,
And in their children's lives is shown
How richly God can bless His own.

Strength for the Inner Self

When John Quincy Adams was an old man, a friend greeted him one day with the familiar words: "How do you do, Mr. Adams?"

The gentleman replied: "John Quincy Adams himself is very well, thank you, but the house in which he lives is falling to pieces. Time and the seasons have nearly destroyed it. I think John Quincy Adams will soon have to move out. But he himself is very well, sir."

Mr. Adams was referring, of course, to his aging body. The passing years had taken their toll on it and soon his immortal soul would take its leave. The apostle Paul put it another way: "Though outwardly we are wasting away, yet inwardly we are being renewed day by day" (2 Corinthians 4:16).

For the child of God there is no dread in the rapid flight of time. The passing years may bring multiple reminders that "swift to its close ebbs out life's little day": the waning strength, the fading vigor, the slowing step, the blurring vision. The years also bring with them the glorious assurances by which our "inner self" is daily renewed.

How avidly the inner self of the maturing Christian feeds on the precious Gospel promises! With each passing year, these promises mean more and more. With each passing year, they pour new strength, new courage, new joy, new hope into the believer's soul.

How could it be otherwise? If God's promises are true (and in Christ all His promises are true), then every passing year brings us that much closer to the complete fulfillment of all God's promises to us—even to our heavenly home.

He who fulfilled His ancient pledges through the miracles of Bethlehem, of Calvary, and of Joseph's garden will surely keep His promise to come again and take us to Himself. Each passing day of our earthly sojourn, therefore, is another day that we have traveled closer to our Father's house.

Small wonder that the believing child of God can say with the great apostle: "Though outwardly we are wasting away, yet inwardly we are being renewed day by day." It is our inner self that daily feeds on the refreshing manna of the promises of heaven.

> Here in the body pent,
> Absent from Him, I roam,
> Yet nightly pitch my moving tent
> A day's march nearer home. (*TLH*)

The Unfinished Sermon

Mr. Matthews was not much of a church-goer. Like many men, he was content to carry his religion in his wife's name. That explained why on a certain Sunday morning he was seated comfortably at home while his wife was attending the Sunday morning service.

Just before noon, a sudden rainstorm blew up from the south. As a caring husband, Mr. Matthews put on his raincoat, grabbed an umbrella, jumped into the family car, and drove to the church two blocks away to pick up his wife.

As he hurried up to the church door, he met a woman who was leaving. "Is the sermon over?" he asked. "No," the woman replied. "The sermon's only half over. The pastor has preached it; now I'm going home to do it."

In a sense, those are the two divisions of every God-pleasing sermon. In the first place, we hear. In the second place, we do something about what we have heard. Too many sermons end after the first part and thus are really never finished. Or to stay with the woman's language, they are never done!

The apostle James had something to say about people who were content to live on unfinished sermons. "Anyone who listens to the word but does not do what it says," James wrote, "is like a man who looks at his face in a mirror and, after looking at himself, goes away and immediately forgets what he looks like" (James 1:23–24).

Looking into a mirror will never remove a blemish from our face, comb our hair, or properly adjust our clothing. The looking must be followed by doing. Listening to sermons Sunday after Sunday will never, in itself, feed the poor, relieve the needy, or bring the comfort of the Gospel to others. There must be a resultant doing.

The plague of much of our church life today is the blight of the unfinished sermon—the sermon that was started by hearing but was never ended by doing. All too frequently the pastor's final "Amen" is misunderstood to mean: "It is finished." In reality, it means: "It is true."

Because the Word that we have heard is true, we can rely on it, and we can go out and act on it—living it each day.

Ask God that, by His grace, we may translate our hearing into fruitful Christian living!

"We Pray to Jesus"

The school nurse had just completed her health talk. There were still a few minutes for a brief review. "Tell me, Jared," she said to a bright-eyed 7-year-old, "what is the first thing we do when we catch a cold?"

Jared replied in confident voice, "We pray to Jesus!"

That wasn't the answer the nurse had expected. For a moment she was at a loss for words, but only for a moment. As she looked into Jared's eager face, she looked into a soul that was filled with faith. Before she knew it, she heard herself replying, "Yes, Jared, we pray to Jesus."

One thing the school nurse knew for sure—Jared came from a Christian home. All the health talks in the world, as beneficial as they may be, could never mean as much to Jared as the Christian faith he had learned at home.

Does your child have that faith? Does he

bring his big little problems to the Savior in prayer? Have you introduced her to the Friend of children? Have you done everything in your power to cultivate an intimate friendship between your child and Christ?

Jesus says, "Let the little children to come to Me ... for the kingdom of God belongs to such as these" (Mark 10:14). Children who have been brought to Christ and kept with Christ will talk to Christ, even about their childhood illnesses.

Our nation knows no starker tragedy than the millions of children who are growing up without learning about their Savior. The church itself can record few darker tragedies than the children in its midst who have only a nodding acquaintance with the Lord who bought them with a price, who have never learned to walk with Him and to talk with Him.

What America needs today is millions of Jareds and Samanthas—children whose parents have brought them to their Savior, who have folded their little hands in prayer, who have accompanied them to church and to Sunday school, and who by word and example have lived the Christian life.

Borne by the Burden

A biologist tells how he watched an ant carrying a piece of straw that seemed almost too heavy for it to drag. The ant came to a crack in the ground that was too wide for it to cross. It stood still for a time, as though perplexed by the situation, then put the straw across the crack and walked over on the straw.

If only we were as wise as that ant! We often speak about the burdens we carry, but have we ever thought of converting our burdens into bridges, of having our burdens bear *us* instead of us bearing *them*?

The apostle Paul learned the secret of being borne by his burden instead of being borne down by it. Throughout his life, Paul had been afflicted with a physical deformity or disability, the exact nature of which we do not know. When he recognized his affliction as part of God's good and gracious will for him, Paul exclaimed: "Therefore I will boast all the more gladly about my weaknesses, so that Christ's power may rest on me. … For when I am weak, then I am strong" (2 Corinthians 12:9–10).

If anyone ever learned how to convert his burdens into bridges, that man surely was the apostle Paul. He took even his stripes and imprisonments and transformed them into open doors through which He shared the Gospel.

We who have found eternal life in the death and resurrection of Jesus Christ can convert our burdens into bridges that lead from the darkness of despair into the brightness of assurance, bridges that lead from a purposeless and drab existence into a life of usefulness and beauty.

Some of the most cheerful and radiant personalities have been those whom God has visited with the greatest crosses. And those who have accomplished the greatest feats in the Father's kingdom have frequently been those who were borne to triumph on the arms of a cross.

To know Christ is to know the love of God, and to know the love of God is to be assured of eternal fellowship with Him. In the light of that assurance, no burden can continue to depress!

Have we learned to know the love of God in Christ? Have we experienced the assurance of His grace? Then He is saying to us, as He once said to Paul, "My grace is sufficient for you, for My power is made perfect in weakness" (2 Corinthians 12:9). With His sustaining grace, we are able to convert all our burdens into bridges.

"Made in Heaven"

You've seen the familiar labels "Made in the U.S.A."; "Made in Japan"; "Made in Germany." Did you know that on every piece of bread that you eat there is an invisible, yet real, label that reads "Made in Heaven"?

Without the hand of God, all the scientific knowledge and skill in the world could not produce a single slice of bread. The formula, the ingredients, the various processes of nature that go into making our daily bread are the property of heaven. How wonderful that a benevolent God is willing to share with us those many priceless blessings for which He alone holds the patent!

We can prepare the soil—God's soil. We can sow the seed—God's seed. We can wait for the rain—God's rain. And we can count on the daily warmth of the sun—God's sun. But without God's soil, God's seed, God's rain, and God's sun, who could create a single head of lettuce or produce a single grain of wheat?

Christ taught us to recognize God's creatorship and ownership when He taught us to pray: "Give us today our daily bread" (Matthew 6:11). The Bible assumes our dependence on God for our daily food when it says: "The eyes of all look to You, and You give them their food at the proper time. You open Your hand and satisfy the desires of every living thing" (Psalm 145:15–16).

It is this recognition that leads Christians to fold their hands before every meal and to offer thanks to heaven. Recognizing the label of heaven, we voice our gratitude to the Owner. Having been restored as sons and daughters of the heavenly Father through faith in Christ, we accept the gifts of heaven as evidence of a Father's love. Christ has made us God's children, and as God's children, we rejoice over every gift that comes from the Father's hand.

What a different place this world would be if we could get our labels straight! The next time you sit down to a meal, trace several of the items on your menu back to their original sources— and rejoice that every one of them was made in heaven!

Light and Shadow

As I flew from Los Angeles to St. Louis, the plane passed over a valley just east of the Sierra Nevada Mountains. As I looked up into endless space, everything was bright and azure blue, to the left and right everything was bathed in brilliant sunshine.

Some miles away, at a level somewhat lower than the plane, drifted a fleecy cloud. From the top, it looked like a downy angel pillow, fluffed, and snowy white with an embroidered edge of gray. Because the cloud was some miles to the left, I also could see the valley that lay beneath it. The valley was a patch of black, a land of shadow shut off from the brilliant sun by the billowy cloud that spread above it.

As the cloud moved slowly southward, the northern edge of the valley began to brighten. I suppose that if my viewpoint could have remained stationary, I soon would have seen the entire valley emerge from the shadow and glow in bright and cheerful colors from the brilliant sun above.

As I looked out of the plane's window, I couldn't help but think about how that valley reminded me of life. For a while, the people living in that valley saw nothing but the cloud—for them there was no sun. Yet I could see that the morning sun was shining brightly. As far as I could see to the left, to the right, ahead, behind, or above, the sun had dispelled the early morning darkness. Only in the valley did it seem that perhaps there was no sun. Yet even there, the inevitable drift of the cloud was beginning to paint the northern slope with the brilliance of the sun above.

There are days when our human shortsightedness causes us to see no evidence of God's sun of love above us. All we see is the blackness of doubt, the shadow of uncertainty, the gloom of distressing foreboding. But that doesn't alter the fact that God's sun of eternal love is fixed and sure.

The love of God, who sent His Son from heaven to earth that someday He might take us from earth to heaven, may be obscured from our human eyes for a season, but it is always there. It is more certain and more lasting than the sun above this earth.

Of one thing we can be forever certain: Above the cloud that hangs above us, the Son of Grace is always shining.

> Judge not the Lord by feeble sense,
> But trust Him for His grace;
> Behind a frowning providence
> Faith sees a smiling face.

"But Calvary Does"

A man who had misspent his life lay critically ill. Turning to his pastor, he asked: "Do you think that a deathbed repentance does away with a whole life of sin?"

"No," the pastor answered quietly, "but Calvary does."

Calvary does away with every sin—the sins of our childhood, the sins of our youth, and those of our old age. "The blood of Jesus, His Son, purifies us from all sin," writes St. John (1 John 1:7). The Lord tells us through the prophet Isaiah: "Though your sins are like scarlet, they shall be as white as snow; though they are red as crimson, they shall be like wool" (Isaiah 1:18). And that means all of our sins!

It's not a question of being late or being early, of being more guilty or less guilty, of being very old or being very young. It's a question of accepting the abundant pardon that is ours through the limitless love of Jesus Christ, our

Savior. There is love for all, there is mercy for all, and there is pardon for all.

Do you feel that you have been harboring some secret sin too long to be forgiven, that you have trampled on God's grace too long to ask for pardon? Take heart! The Scripture tells us that where sin increases, God's love increases all the more. "Now is the time of God's favor, now is the day of salvation" (2 Corinthians 6:2).

The thief on the cross was late—very late—in seeking forgiveness, but not too late! The hour was late in the life of Zacchaeus, but not too late. Both men heard the same message from the lips of the Savior: "Today salvation has come to this house" (Luke 19:9). This day! Have you recognized this day as a day of grace?

> Today Your mercy calls us
> To wash away our sin.
> However great our trespass,
> Whatever we have been,
> However long from mercy
> Our hearts have turned away,
> Your precious blood can wash us
> And make us clean today.

No, nothing that we can do can make up for a whole life of sin. But Christ can. And Calvary does!

His Eye Is on the Sparrow

While raking the grass one evening, I experienced that awful sensation you get when you unexpectedly come across something that is dead. Among the grass clippings beneath the rake, I saw the body of a lifeless sparrow.

For the rest of the evening, that sparrow was on my mind. Again and again, I thought of the Savior's words: "Are not two sparrows sold for a penny? Yet not one of them will fall to the ground apart from the will of your Father" (Matthew 10:29).

Could it be, I mused, that the same God who guides the destinies of His human creations and of nations was concerned about that sparrow? Could this be true? Yes, it could be, it must be, for the Son of God Himself had said so.

If it is true that God cares for sparrows, what does that mean for us? Sometimes it seems that God has passed me by, that I am the only person in the world for whom He has failed to plan and for whom He has failed to make provision.

But our heavenly Father doesn't want me to feel that way. Repeatedly the Savior points to the hand of His Father in the individual lives of Christians. "Your Father knows what you need before you ask Him," He says (Matthew 6:8). He who holds the planets in the hollow of His hand also holds the sparrows. "Don't be afraid; you are worth more than many sparrows" (Matthew 10:31).

Think for a moment of what God already has done for you. Today you eat on the green pastures of His Word and are led beside the still waters of His comforting assurance. This is true because from eternity God saw you out in the desert of sin and decreed that you should be brought into the shelter of His fold. You were lost and would have remained lost forever had His mercy not found you.

But God's mercy did find you! His love did bring you into the safety of the fold. And you can trust that the same Jesus who followed the bitter path of Calvary so He could seek and save His wandering sheep also will care for you and

keep you, now that He has gathered you among
His own.

The God whose eye is on the sparrow surely will not forget those for whom He bled and
died.

> My soul to Thee alone
> Now, therefore, I commend.
> Thou, Jesus, having loved Thine own,
> Wilt love me to the end. (*TLH*)

The Solitary Rose

A traveler was staying at a small-town hotel. As he looked from his second-story window, he saw a gorgeous red rose blooming in a vacant lot next door. It was a single, solitary rose, but somehow it seemed to be all the more beautiful because it stood alone.

As he walked by the vacant lot during the noon hour, he remembered the rose and decided that, if he could find it, he would pick it. But the lot was full of weeds, many of them taller than the rose. From the sidewalk, the man couldn't see the beautiful bloom.

The next morning as he again looked from his second-floor window, there was the same velvety rose, sparkling with diamonds of dew in the rays of the morning sun. From the vantage of his window, he figured the exact position of the rose in the labyrinth of weeds and determined to go down and pick it.

Forcing his way through the thick brush and the almost impenetrable weeds, he finally came to the thin perpendicular stem that held the fragile rose. *How could this rose be growing here?* the man wondered.

Carefully he traced the fragile stem down to the ground, but the stem did not end there. Laboriously he traced the stem as it stretched along the ground amid the weeds. Finally, some distance away, the man found the stem firmly rooted in a cultivated patch of ground in the yard next door. It was there that the bloom got its sustenance!

How very much like the child of God was that single, solitary rose! Frequently God places His children amid the weeds—in the middle of unbelievers. We are not to take on the appearance of the weeds, but we are to give forth the fragrance of the rose and to bloom with refreshing beauty.

The nourishment and strength that makes possible this beauty and this fragrance come from the cultivated patch of ground next door— the life that is "hidden with Christ in God" (Colossians 3:3). It is a life rooted firmly in the Savior. He who said: "I am the vine; you are the branches" (John 15:5) is the source of strength and beauty behind many solitary roses in the weed patches of this world.

"He's My Brother!"

It was dusk on Christmas Eve. As the pastor approached the parsonage, he passed a 12-year-old boy trudging through the snow. He was carrying his 5-year-old brother on his back. The older boy was puffing and his audible breath was visible in the crisp, cold air. It was evident that the burden on his back was almost too much for his youthful shoulders.

"Quite a load for a little boy!" the pastor said and smiled.

Looking at the older man, the red-cheeked boy exclaimed between irregular puffs of breath: "Oh, he ain't heavy, Reverend, he's my brother!"

The pastor stood as if transfixed. As the struggling boy faded into the gray of the gathering dusk, the pastor shook his head. What a theme for a sermon: "He ain't heavy, Reverend, he's my brother!"

What a different world this would be if we

took seriously the deeper implication of Christian kinship, if we were willing to look on every human being as our physical brother or sister, creatures of the same Creator, fit objects for the full measure of our love.

What a different church it would be if we would look on each fellow believer as a brother or sister in Christ. "Keep on loving each other as brothers," the Scriptures admonish us (Hebrews 13:1). "Love the brotherhood of believers," St. Peter encourages (1 Peter 2:17). And to the members of the Lord's family at Galatia, the apostle Paul wrote: "Carry each other's burdens, and in this way you will fulfill the law of Christ" (Galatians 6:2).

Those whose hearts have been warmed and strengthened by a daily consciousness of Christian kinship can carry those who are in need on their shoulders and look at the face of God and say: "He's not heavy, Father, he's my brother! She's not heavy, Father, she's my sister!"

For the eternal miracle that made possible such unselfish love, we return again and again to the manger in Bethlehem and to the cross on Calvary. "This is love," the Bible tells us, "not that we loved God, but that He loved us and sent His Son as an atoning sacrifice for our sins. Dear friends, since God so loved us, we also ought to love one another" (1 John 4:10–11).

Thank God for a Wastebasket!

"A wise use of the wastebasket," said one distinguished editor, "is the secret of all successful editing." Perhaps only those who have spent years doing the work of an editor know how true that observation really is.

A wise use of the wastebasket is not only the secret of successful editing, it is the secret of successful living. Too many lives are encumbered with rubbish that should have been thrown into the wastebasket long ago. Old worries, silly grudges, and smoldering resentments that should have been consigned to oblivion long ago are frequently held on to and nursed along as though we were afraid of losing them.

There is only one place for the petty piques, the festering feuds, and the smoldering grudges of yesterday. That place is in the wastebasket! We don't want the unholy emotions of yesterday to pollute the air of a fresh today or a new tomorrow.

What a difference there would be in family life, congregational life, business life, and public life if each of us had learned to give up unworthy thoughts and base emotions with every setting sun. "Do not let the sun go down while you are still angry," the Bible tells us, "and do not give the devil a foothold" (Ephesians 4:26–27). Rather than give the devil a foothold, we can put the devil in his place!

In another passage of Scripture, we are told: "Let us throw off everything that hinders and the sin that so easily entangles" (Hebrews 12:1). We don't need to carry our pet temptations, our pet prejudices, our pet grievances, and our pet worries from one day to another. With God's help, we can dispose of them.

Those who have learned to "throw off," to "forget," the angry thoughts and base desires that pile up within the heart and to start each new morning unencumbered by a growing backlog of "wrongs to be righted" and "scores to be settled" are truly happy.

The apostle Paul had learned the blessed use of a wastebasket in the nurture of his own spiritual life. Paul says, "Forgetting what is behind and straining toward what is ahead, I press on toward the goal" (Philippians 3:13–14). What an excellent thought at the dawning of each new day! We can ask God to help us forget those things that He would have us forget. We can ask God to help us press forward to those things that He would have us achieve.

Gone with the Wind

The story is told of a woman who confessed to her pastor that she was guilty of the sin of gossip. "What can I do to make amends for the wrong I have done?" she asked.

After a moment's thought, the pastor asked the troubled woman to accompany him into the tower of the church. There he ripped open a pillow filled with goose feathers and exposed the pillow to the wind. Within a few minutes, the pillow was empty. The downy feathers were drifting all over the neighborhood, many of them already beyond the sight of the woman in the church tower.

Turning to the perplexed woman, the pastor instructed her to gather the feathers and to put them back into the pillow.

The assignment was impossible, of course, but no more impossible than it was for the troubled woman to recall the thoughtless words of idle gossip that she had spoken. Like the feathers, the words had spread throughout the town and had gone beyond recall.

It lies in the very nature of slanderous gossip that, as a rule, there is no possible way to make satisfactory amends. If someone steals a dollar, the dollar can be paid back. But if someone starts a vicious rumor, the individual can repent and attempt to stop the rumor's spread, but in reality, the rumor has lodged in a thousand places, most beyond reach.

There may be no way to make restitution for the harm of thoughtless gossip, but, thank God, there is a way of freeing the soul of gossip's guilt. He who remained silent when He died for the sins of all humanity has won for us a glorious pardon, even for those sins when we opened a mouth that should have remained closed.

Surely every one of us has reason to pray:

Oh, let me never speak
What bounds of truth exceedeth;
Grant that no idle word
From out my mouth proceedeth;
And then, when in my place
I must and ought to speak,
My words grant pow'r and grace
Lest I offend the weak. (*TLH*)

"The Heavens Declare"

It was a night flight. I was flying above the clouds. Under the clouds was a town. Above the plane was the diamond-studded canopy of heaven, twinkling with a myriad of stars.

My traveling companion was a learned man. For quite some time, he had impressed me with the various scientific reasons why everything we saw from the plane window could be explained without a God.

When it came my turn for a reply, I was frankly at a loss. It was evident that I could match neither this man's scientific knowledge nor his technical vocabulary. I decided to reply as follows:

> In our basement at home, we have a
> washing machine. At just the right time,
> this machine feeds just the right amount
> of water into the tub—just enough hot
> and just enough cold. At just the right
> time, it sprinkles the clothes with clean,

*warm water for rinsing. At just the right
time, it spins them dry. At just the right
time, it shuts the motor off.*

*Now, which assumption would be more
reasonable: To assume that a lot of bolts
and nuts and washers swirled around in
space until they decided to get together
and become a washing machine, precisely timed and purposefully planned?
Or to assume that behind the washer
there was a mind that conceived the
delicate interrelation of all the various
parts and that brought these parts
together so they would do exactly what
the mind intended?*

As the discussion continued, it seemed my
companion continued to be unimpressed. But
long after that part of the conversation had concluded and we had drifted to another subject,
the man interrupted to observe: "By the way,
I've been thinking about that washing machine
of yours."

As the plane sped on through the night, I
leaned back, looked out the window, and mused:
"The heavens declare the glory of God; the skies
proclaim the work of His hands" (Psalm 19:1).

The Bug on the Windshield

It was a beautiful summer evening, still early enough for me to skim along a scenic highway in Southern Illinois without turning on the lights of the car.

I was in a hurry, so I decided to wait until I got home to clean the splatter from the windshield. As frequently happens on a summer evening, a large bug had collided with the glass, leaving an inelegant blotch to mark the spot of fatal contact.

As I drove along, however, it seemed I couldn't keep my eyes off that ugly spot. I repeatedly found myself focusing on the short-range vision that ended on the pane of glass immediately before me. Each time I fixed my eyes on the ugly spot that was only a matter of inches away, I missed the beautiful panorama that lay before me.

The shades of night were falling as I crested a familiar hill from which on other nights I had seen the shimmer of the evening star. Instead, I saw the splatter of a bug. It was so close, and from my perspective, it was so large, that for a moment, there was no star.

How much this is like life! A bug bigger than the evening star! A bug big enough to blot out the rolling landscape of velvety green that stretched for miles before me! It was all a matter of perspective, of course—a matter of fixing my eyes on the ugly thing that was closest to me while missing the vision of the beautiful that surrounded me.

If only we could keep our eyes off the bugs on our windshields—the doubts and worries that cross our paths, the petty piques, the irritations and vexations, the endless little preoccupations that loom so large in our lives and threaten to blot out the eternal stars of hope and love and faith!

If only we could keep our eyes on Jesus, who is the Way, and on the immovable assurances that He has given us in His eternal Gospel! "I lift up my eyes to the hills—where does my help come from? My help comes from the LORD," writes the psalmist (Psalm 121:1–2).

That is the perspective along which lies the

spiritual landscape of joy and peace and faith and hope. May the Holy Spirit keep our eyes fixed on the hills of God's assurance. May He keep our focus away from the bugs on our windshields.

"Our God Is at Both Ends"

The story is told of a farmer's son who was hauling his first load of hay into town. Perched midway up the mountain of hay that rose high above the wagon—and which bulged out on either side—the young man guided his horses along the country road until he came to a covered bridge.

The bridge was long. Because it was walled in on both sides and covered with a wooden roof, it looked like a dark tunnel.

Pulling his horses to a stop at the bridge's entrance, the boy peered along its inside walls, which seemed to close in funnel-like as they converged on the small patch of light at the other end. Then he turned around and took an appraising look at the broad load he was carrying.

After a moment's deliberation, he shook his head and said, "I'll never make it. The other end's too narrow." So the young man backed up, turned his horses around, and headed toward home.

The boy, of course, was the victim of an optical illusion. Had he gone on, he would have found that the bridge's walls were just as far apart at the far end as they were on his end.

Life is filled with optical illusions. At the entrance to many a new day, as we look along the inside walls of the hours before us, we wonder how we will ever carry our burden past the evening-end of the bridge. But when evening comes, we find that the same Lord who was with us at the entrance to the day was still with us at its close. As we lay the burdens of the finished day aside, we experience the spiritual fulfillment of the prophet's words: "When evening comes, there will be light" (Zechariah 14:7).

How often in the middle of the night, as we look down the dark corridor of the hours before us, has our weak faith almost prayed that the sun would not dawn so our problems would not be put into bold relief by the morning light. Yet when the morning comes, we experience the truth of the psalmist's words: "When I awake, I am still with You" (Psalm 139:18) or our heart has been lifted by the strong assur-

97

ance: "[Your great love is] new every morning" (Lamentations 3:23).

No matter which end of the bridge we stand before, we can be sure: Our God is at both ends! Through Christ we have learned that He is not only the God of power and might and wisdom, but also the God of love and grace and mercy.

No matter which end of the bridge we stand before, God takes our hand in His and helps us move forward courageously.

Crooked Rivers

A little boy who was paging through his first geography book asked his mother: "Why are all the rivers crooked?" The answer, of course, is simple. Rivers are crooked because they follow the paths of least resistance.

The same rule is true of us. Our lives, as a rule, do not become crooked, warped, and out of joint because we deliberately set out to make them that way. Instead, they end up this way because we do not have the courage to overcome the millions of temptations that cross our daily paths.

It's so much easier to listen to gossip than to stop it. It is so much easier to tell a lie than to tell the truth and take the consequences. It's so much easier to stay in bed on Sunday morning than to go to church. It is so much easier to settle down in an easy chair with the evening paper than to go to a Sunday school teachers' meeting or the meeting of the church council or the evangelism committee.

Like the river that meanders around the boulders and skirts the granite ledges to make its lazy way through the unresisting sand, we find it so much easier to do the things that call for the least amount of effort.

Is it any wonder that so many lives are crooked? Is it any wonder that when God looks down from heaven and compares our lives with the perfect rule of His divine commandments that He says: "All have turned aside, ... there is no one who does good, not even one" (Psalm 14:3)? Like the rivers in the geography book, many lives are terribly crooked, turning first to the left and then to the right despite God's commands to move forward.

There is only one hope for a crooked life—a perfect Savior. In Him all crookedness has been forgiven. In Him all crookedness can be made straight and all roughness can be made plain (Isaiah 40:4). To avoid the crookedness and the endless meanderings of life, look to Christ at the dawn of each new day—and ask the Holy Spirit to help you heed His "Follow Me"!

The Canceled Debt

It is said that at one time in his life, Henry Clay owed $10,000 to a bank in Kentucky. A number of sympathetic friends, knowing that Mr. Clay was troubled over his inability to pay, secretly raised the money and paid off the debt.

When Mr. Clay came to the bank to discuss his indebtedness, the cashier startled him with the unexpected announcement: "Mr. Clay, your account has been paid in full!"

"What do you mean?" Mr. Clay exclaimed.

"A number of your friends have raised a sufficient sum and have paid off your debt for you," the cashier said. "You don't owe this bank a dollar."

Tears rushed into Mr. Clay's eyes, and unable to speak, he walked away. His heart was overwhelmed by the joy of a great deliverance—deliverance from a crushing debt.

What a striking illustration of the central fact of our faith. It was just such a deliverance

that St. Paul had in mind when he wrote to the
Christians of his day:

> *When you were dead in your sins …*
> *God made you alive with Christ.*
> *He forgave us all our sins, having*
> *canceled the written code, with its*
> *regulations, that was against us*
> *and that stood opposed to us;*
> *He took it away, nailing it to the cross.*
> Colossians 2:13–14

The written code to which Paul refers was
the Law, which calculated immeasurable debt
of unforgiven sin that stood against us in the
court of heaven. That written code is now gone,
the Bible tells us. It is destroyed, taken away,
canceled! Christ has paid the debt. "God was
reconciling the world to Himself in Christ," Paul
writes, "not counting men's sins against them"
(2 Corinthians 5:19). Because of Christ, God
wasn't charging their sins to their account.

At the foot of Calvary's cross lies the written code that once stood against us. It is blotted
out, its accusations forever covered by the atoning blood of Jesus. From heaven comes the
divine acknowledgment, the receipt that God
Himself has sealed forever by the resurrection

of His Son: "Paid in full! Forgiven through the Savior's blood!"

It was this surpassing knowledge that inspired Horatius Bonar to write those words of humble yet exultant gratitude:

Thy death, not mine, O Christ,
Has paid the ransom due;
Ten thousand deaths like mine
Would have been all too few. (*TLH*)

Are we spending every day of our lives in humble and grateful awareness of God's unmerited forgiveness—of His unbounded love that cancels all our sins?

"Please Do Not Disturb"

I was walking down the eighth-floor corridor of a Hollywood hotel. It was Sunday morning, a little after 9 A.M. On door after door, I saw the familiar placard: "Please do not disturb." I couldn't help thinking of how accurately that little placard expressed the attitude of millions of Americans toward the claims of Christ and His Gospel.

Not only on Sunday mornings, but during every hour of the week, the Son of God stands before human hearts with His age-old invitation and His gracious promise: "Here I am! I stand at the door and knock. If anyone hears My voice and opens the door, I will come in and eat with him, and he with Me" (Revelation 3:20).

Every hour of the week, people respond to this approach of the Savior by pointing to the little placard on the door of their heart: Please do not disturb. They have become so preoccupied with a thousand and one other things in life that they have chosen, consciously or unconsciously, not to be bothered.

But Christ can't be brushed off that easily. If anyone learned this lesson to his complete dismay, it was the Roman governor Pontius Pilate. Nothing would have suited him better on that first Good Friday than to hang out the neat little placard "Please do not disturb." But Jesus was there! Jesus had to be dealt with! A decision had to be made, and it had to be made either "for" or "against."

We may sympathize with a man like Pilate who, when he found himself on the horns of a dilemma, asked again and again: "What shall I do, then, with Jesus?" In the final analysis, that is the question that confronts everyone who comes face to face with the claims of Christ.

The Christ of Christmas, the Christ of Good Friday, and the resurrected Christ of Easter morning is inescapable. No one can hope to remain "undisturbed" by this Christ who was born and lived and died and rose again some 2,000 years ago.

The most happy people in the world are those who have been "disturbed" by the Bible's message of sin and judgment, who have been awakened from their spiritual sleep, and who live in daily awareness of the love of God in Christ Jesus. On the doors of their hearts is inscribed the loving invitation:

Christ Jesus, Lord and Savior, come,
I open wide my heart, Your home.
Oh, enter with Your radiant grace,
On my life's pattern shine Your face.

Pursuing the Trivial

A dog started to chase a bear. Just as the dog came within a few yards of the bear, a fox crossed his path. This turned the dog's attention away from the bear to chase the fox.

When the dog was getting close to the fox, a rabbit ran out from a clump of bushes, and the dog began to chase the rabbit.

By this time the dog was panting hard. But just as he was about to catch the rabbit, a mouse ran into his path. So the dog forgot about the rabbit and began to chase the mouse. He chased it around the field for nearly half a mile when it disappeared into a hole.

Completely exhausted, the poor dog stood at the opening of the hole and barked until he collapsed.

The story is only a parable, of course, but a parable that describes today's busy church. How often do we, at the end of a project that started out to achieve great things for Christ, find ourselves exhausted and barking at a mousehole?

Somehow the big things that we set out to achieve—the high and holy purposes of Christ's kingdom—are successively replaced by smaller things until finally our energies are completely dissipated in the mad pursuit of trivialities.

How many a venture of faith that was born in the prayerful atmosphere of the Upper Room has languished and died in the dirty dishes of the supper room! How many an organization that at its inception was dedicated to the spiritual improvement of its membership has ended up in a stack of dirty silverware and a sinkful of steaming dishwater!

Somewhere along the line, someone got off the track. Like the poor dog who started out to catch a bear, then switched to a fox, then a rabbit, then a mouse before barking himself to death, these groups have permitted their primary objective to be replaced by smaller ones until they have become completely absorbed in secondary aims.

Congregations, church societies, and individual Christians have every reason to emulate the singleness and tenacity of purpose that motivated the apostle Paul. "But one thing I do," he wrote. "Forgetting what is behind and straining toward what is ahead, I press on toward the goal to win the prize for which God has called me heavenward in Christ Jesus" (Philippians 3:13–14).

Those who keep their eyes on the highest goals are not likely to end up pursuing the trivial.

"He Will Be like a Tree"

Have you ever walked down a city street lined with stately sycamores? Rising high on either side of the roadway, like pillars in a huge cathedral, the trees extend their leafy arms across the street to form a canopy of green, affording shade throughout the summer months.

At regular intervals among the sycamores there is a shabby telephone pole—splintered, gashed, and weather-beaten. Although it stands as erect as the sycamores, it sprouts no branches, shoots forth no leaves, and contributes nothing to the gorgeous symphony of green and brown and yellow that thrills those who walk in the shade.

Why the difference? The answer, of course, is simple. The sycamores have roots; the telephone poles have none. The sycamores have tapped an unseen source below the ground from which they draw daily nourishment; the telephone poles are merely lifeless pieces of wood sunk into the ground.

People who have faith in Christ are like those sycamores. Their roots have been sunk into the promises of God. In those promises, believers find the power that transforms life into a fresh, growing, vital thing.

In the familiar words of Psalm 1, one who believes is "like a tree planted by streams of water, which yields its fruit in season and whose leaf does not wither. Whatever he does prospers" (verse 3).

The Savior was doing more than painting a pretty word picture when He said: "I am the vine; you are the branches. If a man remains in Me and I in him, he will bear much fruit" (John 15:5). Those whose lives are firmly rooted in Christ, whose inmost thoughts constantly return to the immovable assurances of the Gospel, are in daily contact with a source of power beyond the ability of mortal humans to fathom.

That is why the leaves of believers do not wither. Like the graceful sycamores whose beautiful leaves also provide shade for the hot and weary traveler, the lives of believers are adorned by the foliage of Christian virtue and will bring comfort and joy to the lives of others.

"Who Taught You to Swear?"

An elderly pastor was riding in the backseat of a horse-drawn coach. The young man who was driving had the habit of swearing at his horses. For some time the clergyman was silent.

Finally, he leaned forward and asked, "Will you tell me, my friend, who taught you to swear? Was it your mother?"

The young man turned toward the pastor with a look of surprise. It was evident the older man had touched a tender spot. "My mother?" replied the driver. "Why, no, sir! My mother is a praying woman. It would break her heart if she ever heard me swearing."

The clergyman then suggested that the driver honor not only the teachings of his Christian mother but also the commandment of his mother's God: "You shall not misuse the name of the Lord your God" (Exodus 20:7).

"Thank you, sir," the young man replied. And during the remainder of the journey not another oath was heard.

Many people, including Christians, need to be reminded that profanity not only dismisses the wishes of Christian mothers, it breaks the Law of God. Cursing and swearing are sinful! Some people may feel they have not achieved full social acceptance until they have learned to curse and swear in public, but profanity actually betrays a limited vocabulary, an emotional immaturity, and a lack of respect for the Word and will of God. Stated simply, to swear is to sin.

James was speaking of the tremendous power of the tongue for good or evil when he wrote: "With the tongue we praise our Lord and Father, and with it we curse men, who have been made in God's likeness. Out of the same mouth come praise and cursing. My brothers, this should not be" (James 3:9–10). Those who have been "purchased for God" (Revelation 5:9) by the death of Jesus Christ, His Son, will not want to use God's name in a disrespectful manner.

A Lantern in the Dark

It was a cold winter's night. Five-year-old Paul held his father's hand tightly as they walked along a dark footpath that led to a neighboring farmhouse.

It was evident that Paul was afraid of the pitch-black darkness that stretched endlessly before him. Finally, looking at the lantern in his father's hand, he whimpered: "Daddy, I'm scared! The light reaches only a little way!"

The father tightened his grip on the little boy's hand and answered with confident assurance: "I know, son. But if we keep on walking, we'll see that the light keeps on shining all the way to the end of the road."

What a fitting parable for Christian pilgrims as we leave another day behind and place our feet on the unknown road ahead! To our heavenly Father, you and I are little Pauls—sometimes confident, but sometimes frightened by the inky darkness that lies ahead.

How often have we whimpered that the light God has given us "reaches only a little way"? Yet we find that if we keep walking in the light that He has given, God's light illuminates each new step we take. God has not given His believers a battery of lights that illuminate each detail of the road ahead. He has given us a lantern in the darkness that, if we follow it, illumines the pathway step by step.

"Your word is a lamp to my feet and a light for my path" (Psalm 119:105). There is no darkness that cannot be pierced by that lamp. In the light of that lamp, we can take each new step with confidence. There may be vast stretches of the road ahead that we cannot see, but the lamp of God's Word assures us that those stretches, just like the step that lies before us, will be illumined by His love.

"If we walk in the light," writes St. John, "as He is in the light, we have fellowship with one another, and the blood of Jesus, His Son, purifies us from all sin" (1 John 1:7). The light of God's lamp is the light of His love. His love, revealed to us in Bethlehem, on Calvary, and again in Joseph's garden, is the guarantee of our security.

"He who did not spare His own Son, but gave Him up for us all—how will He not also, along with Him, graciously give us all things?" (Romans 8:32). Surely, Jesus will be with us, helping us to walk in the light all the way to our heavenly home.

"I Am Still with You"

A Christian woman was taken to the hospital for surgery. Noticing her distress as she was being prepared for the operation, an attendant took her hand and whispered softly:

"You have nothing to fear. Only one of two things could possibly happen to you—both of which are good," the attendant said. "If you die, you will be with Jesus. If you live, Jesus will be with you. In either case, both of you will be together."

What precious comfort! In health or in sickness, in joy or in sorrow, in life or in death, she always would be with Jesus.

King David, whose life was a constant succession of tragedy and triumph, found strength and assurance in that thought. In Psalm 139, he exclaims: "How precious to me are Your thoughts, O God! ... When I awake, I am still with You" (Psalm 139:17–18).

That is our comfort in every dark moment.

That is our comfort especially in the dark moments of illness. The night may be long and trying, the sleep fitful and feverish, the body faint, the heart anxious, but no matter what trials we face, "When I awake, I am still with You." And to be with Christ—what greater comfort could there be?

Even after the night of life's little day is over, when the curtains of eternity are lifted and the Sun of Righteousness beams forth in all His healing brilliance, even in death, "When I awake, I am still with You"!

We don't need to be sick or in trouble or in danger to experience the joy of this constant, unbroken companionship. Every night, when the day's toils are done and the lights are turned out and we lay our head on our pillow to rest, we can close our eyes in the confident assurance that "when I awake, I am still with You."

Nothing in life can harm us because through faith in Christ we are securely held in the Father's hands for all time. He will go with us in every circumstance of life—and in His presence no evil dares to approach us.

Who Puts Up the Numbers?

It happened in a coffee shop in a Chicago hotel. A clergyman was finishing his breakfast when a man slid onto the stool beside him and nervously ordered some rolls and a cup of coffee.

"Did you see that headline?" the stranger asked as he pointed to a bold streamer across the morning paper: *Air Crash Kills 52.* The man continued, "I'm supposed to catch a plane for Los Angeles at noon, and frankly I'm scared stiff. If I didn't have to be there for a meeting in the morning, I'd cancel my reservation and take the train."

As the two men sipped their coffee, they exchanged a few words on the relative safety of travel by air and by train. The clergyman also had a plane reservation that afternoon. He had a ticket for Buffalo, and he intended to use it!

"I guess it's all in the way you look at it," mused the stranger. "When your number's up—it's up."

The minister looked at the frightened man, then replied: "I suppose so. But I happen to know the Man who puts up the numbers."

The stranger put his cup down as though he were afraid he might drop it. Could the minister be joking, or was he serious? Before the man could bring himself to ask, the minister continued. "You see, the Man who puts up the numbers happens to be my Father."

From there, the clergyman told the stranger of the loving care and protection of his heavenly Father, who has promised to protect him always. Both he and his "number" are in the Father's hands—and his number will not be "up" until his Father puts it there.

David, the psalmist, said something very much the same: "My times are in Your hands" (Psalm 31:15). As he looked back at a life that had been lived dangerously, David saw the protecting hand of God in every circumstance. As he looked forward, David knew that the omnipotent hand of his heavenly Father would guide and guard him until his dying day. Maybe that's why David ended the 23rd Psalm with the confident words: "Surely goodness and mercy will follow me all the days of my life, and I will dwell in the house of the LORD forever" (verse 6).

We can have the same assurance. Our lives are in the hands of Him who lived and died that we might live. Those hands will never waver. Someday when our "number is up," we can thank God because He will be holding the number! He will welcome us with open arms to our new home in heaven.

A Study in Pronouns

A grammar lesson about pronouns was being taught at a Christian school. The teacher told the children that a pronoun is a word used instead of a noun.

As an illustration, she asked Mary to read Isaiah chapter 53 and to emphasize the pronouns as she read them. This is what Mary read:

> Surely **He** took up **our** infirmities and carried **our** sorrows, ... **He** was pierced for **our** transgressions, **He** was crushed for **our** iniquities; the punishment that brought **us** peace was upon **Him**, and by **His** wounds **we** are healed. ... The LORD has laid on **Him** the iniquity of **us** all.
> Isaiah 53:4–6

Perhaps Mary didn't realize it, but in those simple words she had delivered the most sublime and the most profound message of all time. The Christian message is, in a sense, a message of pronouns: **He**—for **us**!

"Christ died for **us**," the Scriptures tell us (Romans 5:8). "God made **Him** who had no sin to be for **us**" (2 Corinthians 5:21). "**He** died for all, that **those** who live should no longer live for **themselves** but for **Him** who died for **them** and was raised again" (2 Corinthians 5:15). What blessed pronouns! **He**—instead of **me**!

"God demonstrates **His** own love for **us** in this: While **we** were still sinners, Christ died for **us**" (Romans 5:8). "**He Himself** bore **our** sins in **His** body on the tree" (1 Peter 2:24). "[**He**] loved **me** and gave **Himself** for **me**" (Galatians 2:20).

The Gospel is, above all else, a message of substitution. Christ, the eternal Son of the living God, took our place; He suffered our punishment; He died in our stead; He paid our debt; He secured for us a place in the everlasting mansions of His Father.

> Upon a life I did not live,
> Upon a death I did not die;
> Another's life, Another's death,
> I stake my whole eternity!

His—Twice-Over

The story is told of a boy who spent many days making a sailboat. When the boat was finished, the boy took it to the stream to see if it would sail. Proudly he walked along the riverbank as his little craft glided on the rippling water, its white sail curving in the summer breeze.

But to his consternation, the ship soon headed for the middle of the stream—too far for him to reach. It gradually disappeared from sight. The heartbroken boy returned to his home.

Weeks later, the boy saw what appeared to be his sailboat in a pawnshop window. He went inside and checked it out. Sure enough, it was the same boat he had made and rigged and painted with meticulous care! He asked the owner if he could have the boat, but the man replied: "Only if you pay the price marked on the tag."

For weeks the boy worked to earn the price of the boat. Finally, with the money in his hand, he returned to the pawnshop, placed the money on the counter, and said, "I'd like to have my boat, please."

As he left the store with the boat in his hands, the boy looked at it with pride and joy and affection and said, "You're mine, little boat! You're mine twice-over! Once because I made you; twice because I bought you!"

The analogy may be imperfect, as most analogies are, but the way the boy felt about his boat is the way God feels about us. The Bible says: "It is He who made us" (Psalm 100:3). It also tells us: "You were bought at a price" (1 Corinthians 6:20). It even tells us about the price that was paid to buy us back: "You were redeemed [bought back] ... with the precious blood of Christ" (1 Peter 1:18–19).

What a comfort to know that we have a Father in heaven who looks at us and says: "You are Mine. You are Mine twice-over. Once because I made you; twice because I bought you."

A Sermon
from a Train Window

I was traveling by train from Los Angeles to St. Louis. The floodwaters in the Midwest had reached a new high. Farmlands and highways lay beneath a murky lake that stretched as far as my eyes could see.

Slowly and cautiously, the train made its way into what seemed to be a trackless and bottomless lake. Would it sink? Would it lose its way? Was it headed for disaster?

Confidently the engineer headed the nose of the engine into the swirling waters. He knew that only a few inches below the surface of the flood were solid tracks—invisible to the eye but there nonetheless. Because he had traveled this way a hundred times before, he knew the unseen tracks would hold the train above the water and lead to dry land just a mile or two ahead.

As the passengers looked from the train windows, we were startled by the illusion of a heavy passenger train sailing gracefully across the surface of the surging flood!

I was reminded of the word of Scripture: "The eternal God is your refuge, and underneath are the everlasting arms" (Deuteronomy 33:27). Underneath the train were the solid roadbed, the sturdy ties, the heavy spikes, and the unbending rails of steel.

Those of us who have found forgiveness for our sins through faith in Jesus Christ can launch out upon a trackless future, confident that "underneath are the everlasting arms." We know that, through Christ, the almighty God has become our strong Protector. The floodwaters of adversity, the storms of trial, the winds and waves of distress may threaten to throw us off course, but we are riding on solid tracks. These tracks have been forged and fashioned by God Himself and lead through the gathering waters to the safe, dry land of heaven.

The everlasting arms that are always underneath can be seen only through the eyes of faith. But we who have once seen them can walk, even on the floods!

Revealed by His Footprint

Martin and Christopher were spending a week on the Appalachian Trail. Day after day, Christopher spent time each evening talking with God.

At last, one evening when Christopher came back from his prayer time, Martin asked, "How do you know there *is* a God?"

Christopher fixed his eyes on his friend, then replied, "How do I know there *is* a God? I'll answer that question if I can ask you one first. How did we know this morning that it was a fox and not a bear that had passed our tent while we slept?"

Martin laughed. "We could tell by the paw print in the dirt."

Christopher then looked to the west where the setting sun threw shafts of red and gold and purple into the vaulted canopy of heaven. Pointing toward the sun, he said, "Neither is that the footprint of a man."

The world around us is filled with the footprints of God. Every sunset, every sunrise, every twinkling star in the diamond-studded ceiling that envelopes this marvelous world is a footprint of our Maker.

The Bible tells us: "The heavens declare the glory of God; the skies proclaim the work of His hands" (Psalm 19:1). The person who can see the scarlet sun sink into a pool of purple, splashing the sky with streaks of gold and crimson, and still not see the footprint of the Maker is like a pair of spectacles without a pair of eyes behind them.

But God has not left us to follow the path to Him by following footprints. He has revealed Himself to us through the pages of His Word. The book of nature may tell us that there is a God, but only the Book of Books can tell us who He is and what He has done for us through Jesus Christ, His Son.

The footprints of the setting and the rising sun may tell us that God *is*. Only the nailprints in the hands of our Redeemer can tell us that God is Love.

Not Better—But Better Off

A soldier was making fun of his buddy who was a sincere believer in Christ. "The trouble with you Christians," said the scoffer, "is that you think you are better than the rest of us."

"Not better," replied the Christian young man, "just better off."

How true! Those who have been brought into a right relationship with God through faith in Christ are indeed better off than those who have not. People who have become "new" in Christ and who lead Christian lives by the power of the Holy Spirit are much better off than those who turn their backs on the Gospel and determine to "go it alone."

"Godliness has value for all things," the Bible tells us, "holding promise for both the present life and the life to come" (1 Timothy 4:8). Believers don't have to wait until heaven to be better off—we are better off here and now! While God has not told us that godliness holds promise of material success, He has told us that the rewards of humble trust in Christ are peace, joy, assurance, the victorious inner life, and, finally, eternal life with Him in heaven.

To know every morning that we have a Savior who has promised to be with us always, even to the end of the world (Matthew 28:20), and to know every evening that we have a Savior who has died to restore us as heirs of His Father—such knowledge is indeed a blessing for which we have no measurement.

Our daily sins may convince us that we are no better than anyone else, but God's daily grace convinces us, beyond all doubt, that we are better off!

It was this knowledge that prompted the poet to write:

> Perish ev'ry fond ambition,
> All I've sought or hoped or known;
> Yet how rich is my condition!
> God and heav'n are still my own. (*TLH*)

To Heaven on a Pass?

John had put the question somewhat irreverently, but the question hit the mark: "Do you mean that I can get to heaven on a pass?"

Somewhat surprised at this unusual language, the pastor thought for a while, then replied: "Yes, John. In fact, that is the only way you can get there. There are no 'paid admissions.' Whoever gets to heaven gets there on a pass."

"But that just isn't reasonable," John responded.

"I know," said the clergyman and smiled. "God didn't consult us in arranging His plan of salvation. We should be thankful for that. I'm sure none of us would have thought of a plan as wonderful as His.

"Even the apostle Paul couldn't figure out all the whys and wherefores that lay behind God's marvelous plan," the pastor continued. "That's why he wrote: 'Oh, the depth of the riches of the wisdom and knowledge of God! … Who has known the mind of the Lord? Or who has been His counselor?' (Romans 11:33–36).

"But let's come back to your somewhat unusual expression once more," said the pastor. "St. Paul wrote an entire book of the Bible, the epistle to the Romans, to show that no one could possibly 'buy a ticket' to heaven. That is, no one could possibly get there through personal effort, personal goodness, or personal morality.

"In fact, Paul claimed that no one could even make a partial payment on the ticket or cooperate with God in any way in the purchase of salvation. He said that entrance into heaven was only 'by pass,' only by grace, only by trusting the shed blood of Jesus Christ, God's Son. It's in Romans 3:20–28, which says …"

We may not be ready to use John's language about getting to heaven on a pass, but his question showed that he understood the Christian doctrine of justification by faith. This doctrine says we get to heaven not because of any merit of our own, but solely through faith in the substitutionary life and death and resurrection of the Savior.

Just as I am, without one plea
But that Thy blood was shed for me
And that Thou bidd'st me come to Thee,
O Lamb of God, I come, I come.

The Practice of His Presence

The story is told of a pious Scotsman who was suffering from a critical illness. One day he was visited by the new minister who had only recently been called to the parish.

After the pastor had seated himself by the sick man's bedside, he noticed a vacant chair pulled up on the other side of the bed. Evidently it had been used just before he entered the room.

Pointing to the vacant chair, the pastor said: "Well, I see I'm not your first visitor this morning."

Following the pastor's eye to the vacant chair, the man replied: "That chair? Let me tell you about it. Many years ago, I found it impossible to pray when I went to bed. I often fell asleep on my knees because I was so tired. If I managed to keep awake, I couldn't keep my thoughts from wandering.

"One day I spoke to the minister about it,"

the man said. "He told me not to worry about kneeling down. 'Just sit on your bed,' he said, 'and put a chair opposite you. Imagine that Jesus is in it, and talk to Him just as you would to a friend.'

"I began doing that," the man continued, "and I've been doing it ever since. Now you know why the chair is there like that."

It wasn't many days later when the old man's daughter came to the minister's home. "Father died last night," she said, tears moistening her cheeks. "I had no idea death was so near. He seemed to be sleeping so comfortably. When I went back to see if everything was all right, he was dead.

"He hadn't moved since I saw him a few minutes before," she explained, "except that his hand was lying on the empty chair at the side of his bed."

It may not be possible for us to cultivate the habit of the vacant chair, but how important it is that each of us cultivate the practice of the Savior's presence. In life and in death, we will be blessed beyond measure if our hand is in His.

Each morning and again each night, we can consciously put our hand in His. Then we will be able to say with the psalmist: "Even though I walk through the valley of the shadow of death, I will fear no evil, for You are with me" (Psalm 23:4).

What a Friend!

The teacher was leading her class in a study of definitions. She read the words, and the children would take turns giving their own definitions.

It seemed all the children were well prepared on this particular morning. One after another gave a definition of uncle, aunt, cousin, neighbor—much to the delight not only of the teacher, but also of the whole class, which took pride in the group achievement.

When Sarah's turn came, however, it looked for a moment as though their splendid record would be broken. Sarah was the first student to hesitate and to fumble. The word that she had been given to define was *friend.* Simple as it might be, Sarah could think of no way to define this familiar word.

Finally, after desperate mental effort, she blurted out her childlike definition of a friend. "A friend," she said, "is someone who likes me, even though he knows me!"

Perhaps Sarah's definition won't be included in any dictionary, yet it contains insights that aren't contained in many formal definitions of *friend.* Isn't a part of the essence of friendship that one person continues to "like" the other despite evident faults and shortcomings? Truly, a friend is someone who likes us, even though he knows us!

How true that is especially of the friendship that exists in the heart of God and that goes out to all His fallen creatures. He knows us for what we are, yet He loves us. Indeed, no one knows us better nor loves us more.

St. Paul tells us that "God demonstrates His own love for us in this: While we were still sinners, Christ died for us" (Romans 5:8). In the very same chapter, we are told that Christ died for those whom He knew to be ungodly.

If it is true, as Sarah said, that "a friend is someone who likes me, even though he knows me," then what a friend we have in Jesus!

Jesus knows our every weakness, yet His heart goes out to us in pity, compassion, and affection. He who said, "Greater love has no one than this, that he lay down his life for his friends" (John 15:13) proved the immeasurableness of His love by dying even for His enemies!

What a Friend!

Barging In on Christmas?

It was a cold November morning. Two women, their arms filled with bundles and their coat collars turned up against the wind, were walking past the window of a large downtown department store.

In the window was a life-size tableau of the Nativity scene: the Christ Child in the manger, Mary and Joseph, the kneeling shepherds, and cattle standing nearby.

"Imagine that!" one woman said. "The churches are even barging in on Christmas!"

To her, the substitution of the Christ Child for Kris Kringle was an unwarranted intrusion by the religious community. What irony that the world should have drifted so far from the original significance of the Christmas season that the King of kings should be accused of "barging in" on His own birthday party!

What the world needs is more—and not less—of such "barging in." During the

141

Christmas season, we can remind people that the message of the season is a missionary proclamation: "I bring you good news of great joy that will be for all the people" (Luke 2:10).

All people, including the millions of busy shoppers who are milling through the crowded aisles of department stores, need to be told that a Savior has been born for them. They need the church to "barge in" on their preoccupation with the toys and tinsel of the season. And we can't deny that many Christian homes would benefit from the church and its message of pardon and peace through the Christ Child taking a more important part in the family celebration.

Will yours be just another X-mas celebrated with the triple *X* of extravagance, excitement, ant exhaustion? Or will it be a truly Christian *Christ*mas celebrated in the company of Him whose birth we commemorate? It will be the latter in the measure in which the Honored Guest of Christmas occupies your hearts—at home, at church, at work, and at play.

Christ Jesus, Lord and Savior, come,
I open wide my heart, Your home.

Mount Sin and Mount Grace

Have you ever driven along a highway next to a mountainside? As you looked up, you could see nothing but mountain. It seemed the steep ascent was endless. An hour later, when you were 50 or 60 miles away, you looked back and saw the mountain in its true perspective. Towering high above it, still farther in the background, rose a majestic mountain peak that literally dwarfed the mountain that had looked so large when you were so close.

There is a spiritual counterpart to this in the life of every Christian. As we look back over the path we have traveled in the past year, there loom before our eyes two great mountain peaks: the mountain of our sin and the mountain of God's grace.

Mount Sin is always there. How we hate it! How we deplore it! We must confess to our shame that the past has again been a year of many grievous sins. Standing high on the horizon that stretches out behind us is the frightening heap of our accumulated transgressions.

Towering high above this mountain, unexcelled in glory and in grandeur, is the thrilling sight of Mount Grace. Our sins during the past year may have been great, but God's grace has been even greater. The ugly stain of our sin may have spread far and wide, but the healing shadow of His overpowering grace has spread even farther.

In the same way the smaller mountain melts away in the shadow of the greater, Mount Sin is forever being swallowed up in the shadow of Mount Grace. In the shadow of God's grace, all sin disappears.

In a sense the apostle Paul was speaking of Mount Sin and Mount Grace when he wrote to the Christians in Rome: "Where sin increased, grace increased all the more" (Romans 5:20). Sin was great, but grace was greater!

Therefore, we can cross the threshold of the new year with these two all-pervading thoughts: deep repentance for our personal sin and humble trust in divine grace. While we experience absolute despair of our own record of accomplishment, we have absolute and unwavering confidence in our Savior, whose record of accomplishment has been written to our credit and who will be our Savior in the new year even as He has been in the old.

This Side of Heaven

As I write these lines, I am seated at the window of a speeding Pullman car crossing the plains of Wyoming. It is late and almost time to retire. A few moments ago I was sitting alone in the darkness of the room, looking out into the blackness that has fallen like a shroud on the world.

The night is clear, and the sky is a shimmering vault of velvet with myriads of tiny windows, as it were, that let bits of light peek through from a land that knows no night. As I looked out of the window, I thought of a little girl, who, reflecting on the splendor of a summer sky, said to her father, "Daddy, if the wrong side of heaven is so beautiful, how wonderful the right side must be!"

No human tongue or pen has ever succeeded in describing the glory, the grandeur, and the magnificence of the Father's house above. That it is a place of entrancing beauty and matchless splendor the apostle John indicates in the book of Revelation. He interprets heaven's glories in terms of costly jewels, precious gems, and rarest metals.

How could heaven be anything else but beautiful! It is the habitation of our God, the royal palace of our King! And in that palace, our Savior has gone to prepare a place for us. Through faith in Him, we will ascend someday to His beautiful home beyond the skies, a place more exquisite, more glorious, more wonderful than human speech can tell!

As the train speeds on into the night, I know there is someone up front who will stay awake and bring us safely to our destination. In a moment, I will put away the typewriter and retire for the night. But before I close my eyes, I will look once more to the shining windows of heaven and pray:

> Lord Jesus, since You love me,
> Now spread Your wings above me
> And shield me from alarm.
> Though Satan would devour me,
> Let angel guards sing o'er me;
> This child of God shall meet no harm.

Standing on God's Promises

In the early days of our country, a weary traveler came to the banks of the Mississippi River for the first time. There was no bridge. It was early winter, and the surface of the mighty stream was covered with ice. Could he cross over? Would the uncertain ice bear his weight?

Night was falling, and it was urgent that he reach the other side. Finally, after much hesitation and with much fear, he began to creep cautiously across the frozen surface on his hands and knees. He thought this approach might distribute his weight more evenly and keep the ice from breaking beneath him.

About halfway over he heard the sound of singing behind him. Out of the dusk came a man driving a horse-drawn load of coal across the ice. He was singing merrily as he went on his way! The man on the ice looked at his trembling hands, his fear that the ice would not be strong enough to bear his weight still fresh in his mind.

Then he looked again at the driver, the heavy load, and the horses traveling across the same ice!

Like this weary traveler, some of us have learned only to creep along on the promises of God. Cautiously, timidly, with much trembling, we venture forth as though the lightness of our step might make God's promises more secure. As though we could ever contribute even in the smallest way to the strength of God's assurances!

God has promised to be with us. We can believe that promise. He has promised to uphold us. We can believe what He says. He has promised to grant us victory over all our spiritual enemies. We can trust His truthfulness. Above all, He has promised to grant us full and free forgiveness of all our sins because of Jesus Christ. And He has promised to take us to His heavenly home. We can take Him at His Word.

We don't have to creep on these promises as though they were too fragile to hold us. We can stand on them, confident that God is as good as His Word and that He will do what He has pledged. It was this thought that the apostle Paul had in mind when he wrote to the Corinthians: "Stand firm in the faith; be men of courage; be strong" (1 Corinthians 16:13). Don't creep.

A Friend
in the Father's House

Few memories of childhood are more vivid in later years than those melancholy moments when, having offended a parent by some childish misdemeanor, we are "afraid to go home."

What will Dad say? What will Mom do? Would there be any escape from the punishment? If only someone, maybe a sister or brother, would take our side. If only someone would put in a good word for us and would encourage Mom or Dad to forgive and to forget. If only there were someone who understood!

There is such a person in our Father's house above. At this very moment, He is "taking our side." At this very moment, He is "putting in a good word for us." At this very moment, He is pleading with His Father (and ours) to forgive us.

This friend in the Father's house, of course, is Jesus. "My dear children," writes John, "if anybody does sin, we have one who speaks to the Father in our defense—Jesus Christ, Righteous One" (1 John 2:1). Hebrews tells us more about this great friend of sinners: "He is able to save completely those who come to God through Him, because He always lives to intercede for them" (Hebrews 7:25).

On Calvary's cross, while dying for the sins of all humanity, Jesus exclaimed: "Father, forgive them" (Luke 23:34). He still looks down in love on His believing children and still is pleading before His Father's throne on high: "Father, forgive them"!

All our worries, all our anxieties, all our fears that stem from a guilty conscience and that make us afraid to step into the holy presence of our heavenly Father can be put to rest. Next to our Father's throne stands our Elder Brother. He has suffered and died that we might live. He has risen again and ascended to His home on high where He puts in an eternal word for us!

He lives to bless me with His love;
He lives to plead for me above; …
He lives to calm my troubled heart;
He lives all blessings to impart.

"It Fits Them All!"

Linda's eyes were big as saucers as she leaned on the kitchen table and exclaimed, "Oh, Mama! It fits them all!"

She had been kneeling on a chair next to the table, watching her mother pour jelly into an assortment of containers—jelly glasses, Mason jars, tumblers, and even a stemmed goblet that had been in the family for years.

To Linda's active mind it was nothing short of a miracle that the formless liquid her mother was ladling from the large kettle could assume the exact form of each container, from the smallest glass to the largest jar. In her excitement, she cried, "Oh, Mama! It fits them all!"

So, too, does God's grace fit every day in the life of the believer. Our days are like Linda's mother's assortment of containers—no two are alike. Some of our days are twisted grotesquely by disappointment and discouragement. Some are flat with the monotonous humdrum of colorless routine. Some are high with spiritual adventure and achievement. Some are deep with doubt and dark despair.

But God's grace is sufficient for all of them (2 Corinthians 12:9). His grace floods every corner of our lives. His grace takes the shape of each new day because He has promised that our strength will equal our days (Deuteronomy 33:25).

There is not a single corner of our lives—no matter how small, how secret, or how secluded—into which God's healing love won't flow. Indeed, it is part of the miracle of God's grace that, after it has flooded and filled each new day, there is always some left over. The apostle Paul tells us: "Where sin increased, grace increased all the more" (Romans 5:20).

Not only does the love of God fill our every day according to its needs, but as each succeeding day is finished and ready to be put away, God's love is still there, ready to fill the next. Therefore we need not be fearful of tomorrow. When tomorrow's sun dawns, God's grace will still be able to fill our every need—"It fits them all!"

"If I Would Love Him More"

An eminent artist spent weeks painting a life-size picture of the Savior. As he was adding the last delicate touches to the Master's face, a woman entered the workroom. Standing at a distance, she watched him in silence.

When the artist became aware of her presence, the woman broke her silence and remarked, "You surely must love Him!"

Stepping back from his work and looking at it almost wistfully, the painter replied: "Love Him? Indeed I do!" After a moment's hesitation, he added: "But if I would love Him more, I would paint Him better!"

In a very real sense, it is part of the Christian's calling to "paint Christ" for others. St. Peter writes: "You are a chosen people, a royal priesthood, a holy nation, a people belonging to God, that you may declare the praises of Him who called you out of darkness into His wonderful light" (1 Peter 2:9).

It is the very purpose of Christ's people that they declare the praises of their Redeemer amid unbelievers. Through word and deed, we acquaint others with the wonders of Christ's love and the redeeming power of His death on the cross.

What picture of the Savior are you painting for your friends and neighbors, those whom see you daily? Is it the picture Jesus would have us paint? Or is it a caricature of the Lord of glory?

Perhaps some of us will confess with the artist: "If I would love Him more, I would paint Him better." If I would love Him more deeply, live with Him more intimately, speak to Him more frequently, listen to Him more attentively, obey Him more implicitly, then I would reflect the power of His love more radiantly and more gloriously.

Indeed, each of us might well fix the eyes of our faith on the Christ whom we adore, and pray:

> Beautiful Savior, King of creation,
> Son of God and Son of Man!
> Truly I'd love Thee, Truly I'd serve Thee,
> Light of my soul, my joy, my crown.

Mission Sermon on the Mount

I stood high on a mountain overlooking the sprawling city of Los Angeles. Beneath me, spreading as far to the left and to the right as I could see, lay a sight that defies description.

Like necklaces of shimmering jewels, the lights of the city sparkled brightly against the velvety black of a summer's night. There was no sound, yet in the distance I could see thousands of tiny lights moving slowly in all directions, criss-crossing one another in a dazzling tapestry of light and darkness.

These tiny distant lights were cars—each going somewhere at this late hour, each carrying precious human cargo. In the vast patches of black between the golden strands were darkened homes, invisible and silent. In these homes were people, many of them asleep.

As I stood there, I thought about those words of Scripture recorded in the gospel of Luke: "As He approached Jerusalem and saw the city, He wept over it" (Luke 19:41). There was something somber, something melancholy, about that sight.

Of the millions of people whose frantic lives were being lived on the glittering stage that stretched before my view, how many were living in the darkness of spiritual night? How many were sleeping the sleep of spiritual death? How many were prepared to meet their God?

I thought, too, of God's description of this darkened world and of the great command that He has given to the members of His church: "Arise, shine," He says, "for your light has come, and the glory of the LORD rises upon you. See, darkness covers the earth and thick darkness is over the peoples, but the LORD rises upon you and His glory appears over you" (Isaiah 60:1–2).

Twenty-four hours have passed since I stood on that mountain, but somehow the picture and the message remain. To me, it will always be my mission sermon on the mount.

A Funeral Wreath
in Heaven?

At one time in his life, Martin Luther was extremely depressed and found it difficult to conceal his melancholy mood. Soon he noticed that his wife, Kate, had put on her mourning garments and had adopted an unaccustomed attitude of somber silence.

When he asked the reason for this sudden change, Kate replied, "From the way you've been acting, I thought that God had died. I thought it proper that I should go in mourning."

We often seem to go about our daily tasks as though there were a funeral wreath on our Father's house above, as though our heavenly Father had died and left us to fend for ourselves as best we could! We often plod along our pilgrim path as though our Father's house were empty, as though there were no living, loving Father there to care for us, to guide us, and to shield us with His mercy!

In days of sorrow and adversity, in days of problems and perplexities, we can remember that through Christ we have become the children of the *living* God. We are God's children, not His orphans!

The Scriptures tell us that our God is in the heavens and that nothing is impossible with Him. He who gave us the choicest jewel of heaven, His only begotten Son, will also give us those few temporal gifts we need to support and sustain our earthly life. He who charts the courses for the sun, the moon, the stars will also find a path for us.

No, there is no funeral wreath in heaven. Our Father is still in His house. Because He is, our Savior tells us: "Do not set your heart on what you will eat or drink; do not worry about it. ... Your Father knows that you need them" (Luke 12:29–30).

> Lord, give us such a faith as this;
> And then, whate'er may come,
> We'll taste e'en now the hallowed bliss
> Of an eternal home. (*TLH*)

"Such a Little Way Together"

They were at the supper table. Carl was telling about an exasperating experience he had on the way home from work.

"This woman got on the bus at 55th," he said, "and squeezed into a small space right beside me. There she sat, half on top of me. Her packages poked me in the face constantly. I had to keep dodging so one box wouldn't knock my glasses off."

Carl's son piped up: "Why didn't you tell her that she was half on your seat and that she should get up?"

"It wasn't worthwhile" replied Carl. "We had such a little way to go together."

Carl didn't realize it, but he had expressed a theological thought that might serve as a motto for all of us: "It wasn't worthwhile. We had such a little way to go together."

How relatively unimportant the vexations and irritations of the day become when we view them in their true perspective. The unkindness, the ingratitude, the lack of understanding on the part of others becomes easier to bear when we remember that "we have such a little way to go together."

It also becomes more urgent that we show patience, forbearance, and reasonableness to those who are making life's journey hand in hand with us. After all, "we have such a little way to go together."

We have so little time to show the virtues of Him who has called us out of darkness into His wonderful light! So little time to demonstrate the love of Him who first loved us! So little time to live His Gospel!

What a different world this would be, what a different church it would be, what a different family we would have if each of us would remember: We have such a little way to go together!

The Wrong Start

"Mommy, my coat's wrong!" Four-year-old Beth had been struggling valiantly with the buttons on her new winter coat. Finally, after great effort, she thought she was finished. She had successfully poked each button through a hole. To her surprise and dismay, there was still a buttonhole left over! In her childish reasoning, she concluded that whoever had made the coat had made a mistake.

There had been a mistake all right, but the mistake was not the coatmaker's. It was Beth's. She had poked the first button into the wrong hole, and of course, every button after that was wrong.

Beth had to be taught the importance of that very first button. If she put that one into its proper place, all the rest would be comparatively simple. Beth's mother learned something too. There were a lot of other things in life in which it was important that Beth avoid the wrong start.

It is always possible to unbutton a coat and to start over; it is not always possible to unbutton a life and to make a new beginning.

The habits Beth was forming as a child would establish the pattern of her future habits. If these habits are wrong, it's best to correct them immediately. It will be much more difficult later.

Christian parents know how important it is for their children to "get that first button right." They realize the truth of the scriptural command and promise: "Train a child in the way he should go, and when he is old he will not turn from it" (Proverbs 22:6). That is why they teach their children about Christ and surround them with a wholesome Christian influence throughout their childhood. That is why they seek to place their children's feet on the path of faith and righteousness as early in life as possible.

With God's help, they want to give their children the right start.

God's Evergreens

On a wooded hillside in southern Illinois stood a mammoth evergreen. In the springtime, when other trees were dressing themselves in their Easter finery, this evergreen seemed out of place. In the noontime of summer it was so much like the trees around it that it seemed to be lost in the landscape. And when autumn decked its neighbors in gorgeous garments of gold and red and purple, it seemed to be the most drab and lifeless of all the trees on the hillside.

But when winter arrived and the other trees, stripped of their foliage, were waving skeleton arms in the wind, then the humble evergreen stood out in all its verdant beauty. Even with the snow bending its drooping boughs, it was just as green, just as graceful, as it had been in the full flush of summer.

As I drove along the winding highway that skirted the edge of the hillside, I often thought about how strikingly that evergreen symbolized the spiritual vigor and vitality of the Christian life.

The believer in Christ is one of God's evergreens "whose leaf does not wither" (Psalm 1:3). In the winter life, when the winds blow stiff and strong, when the dull gray skies of gloom and sorrow shut out the rays of cheering sunshine, we stand out as God's evergreens.

The source of our strength is God's love, and God's love knows no spring or summer or autumn or winter. It is ever constant, ever availing. With God's love, as with God Himself, there is no change or variableness. He has revealed His love to us through Jesus Christ, who is the same yesterday, today, and forever.

Come sunshine or sorrow, good fortune or calamity, delight or distress, Christians have found a source of spiritual nourishment unknown to others. Their roots have been sunk deep into the promises of God. From these assurances, we draw daily strength to adorn our lives with Christian virtues no matter what the circumstance.

Believers in Christ are indeed God's evergreens.

The Best Translation

Four clergymen were discussing the relative merits of the various translations of the Bible. One liked the King James Version best because of its beautiful, classical English. Another liked the American Revised Version best because it is more literal and comes closer to the original Hebrew and Greek. The third had a strong preference for the Revised Standard Version because, as he put it, "it speaks the language of our day and is much more understandable."

The fourth minister, not quite ready to express a preference, remained silent. When he was pressed for his opinion, he surprised his colleagues with the statement, "I like my mother's translation best."

He didn't mean to express an indifference toward the respective merits of the various versions his friends were discussing, but he did want to make an important point. It is possible for theologians to translate the original languages of the Bible into our modern idiom without ever translating its teachings into practice. It was this latter art that his mother had mastered.

Through her noble Christian life, she had translated the Scriptures into something he could read, even as a child. Her love, her patience, her gentleness—these were her "translations" of the great scriptural injunctions that she wanted to pass on to her children.

In that sense, each of us is a translator of the Bible. By our consistent Christian life, we "translate" the Bible's message to those who will never take the time to read the written Word. Whether or not we like it, we are the only Bibles that many people will read. Are we reliable "translations"?

In a very real sense, the Savior was asking each of us to be a relayer of God's message to others when He said: "Let your light shine before men, that they may see your good deeds and praise your Father in heaven" (Matthew 5:16). Are we "translating" His message?

God's Go-Between

During World War I, a French officer fell wounded in front of the French trenches. The enemy's shrapnel was bursting all around him as he lay entirely unprotected.

Seeing the danger, a private crawled out of the trench, dressed the officer's wounds as best he could, and lying down beside him, whispered in his ear: "Do not fear! I am between you and the shells. They must hit me first."

What a beautiful picture of Jesus, who on Calvary's cross placed Himself between us and the thunderbolts of God's justice. As our Savior hung there on that instrument of torture, it was as if He were saying to you and to me: "Do not fear! I am between you and the strokes of divine justice. They must hit Me first."

Jesus is the eternal go-between. He is the mediator between God and humanity. As the Scriptures tell us: "There is one God and one mediator between God and men, the man

Christ Jesus" (1 Timothy 2:5).

By His sinless life and by His holy, innocent suffering and death in the sinner's stead, Jesus has taken His place between us and the stern demands of God's consuming justice. We don't have to fear because Jesus was "pierced for our transgressions, He was crushed for our iniquities; the punishment that brought us peace was upon Him, and by His wounds we are healed" (Isaiah 53:5).

"Do not fear! I am between you and the shells. They must hit me first." What glorious assurance when we hear these words translated into their spiritual significance and uttered by our Redeemer. What wonderful comfort! With such a Savior at our side, there is nothing in life or in death that can harm us. At the opening and closing of each day, we can lift our eyes to Him and pray with confident assurance:

Cover my defenseless head
With the shadow of Thy wing.

The Place for Burdens

An elderly woman was one of several passengers in the express elevator as it left the downstairs lobby and headed for the 20th floor.

It was late afternoon, and it was evident that she was exhausted. She stood in the center of the elevator, her shoulders drooping with the weight of the two heavy bundles she was carrying—one in each hand.

Another passenger, a young woman, turned to the older woman and said, "You can put your bundles down, ma'am. The elevator will carry them."

Somewhat sheepishly, but nevertheless gratefully and with an audible sigh of relief, the older woman dropped her two bundles to the floor and let the elevator carry them.

What a picture of how many Christians carry their burdens. We believe with all our hearts that "underneath are the everlasting arms," but we prefer to carry our own burdens.

The psalmist tells us: "Cast your cares on the LORD and He will sustain you" (Psalm 55:22). Peter admonishes, "Cast all your anxiety on Him because He cares for you" (1 Peter 5:7). And Moses reminds us: "The eternal God is your refuge, and underneath are the everlasting arms" (Deuteronomy 33:27).

Surely, the omnipotent power that sustains us and that carries us from day to day will be able to carry our burdens too. Through Christ and His sacrificial death on the cross, we have learned that the omnipotent God is the God of love and infinite compassion. Should we be afraid to cast our burdens on such a God?

The elevator was strong enough to carry the woman and her bundles—whether they were in her arms or on the floor. And the God of heaven is strong enough to carry us and our burdens—whether we insist on carrying them ourselves or cast them on Him.

Remember—It was to the burden bearers that the omnipotent Son of Heaven once said: "Come to Me, all you who are weary and burdened, and I will give you rest" (Matthew 11:28). Give Christ your burdens; in exchange He will give you rest!

A Birthday Gift for Daddy

Aunt Martha was visiting at the home of her niece Jessica. When Jessica's father left the living room, the little girl whispered to her aunt that she was going to give her daddy a pair of slippers for his birthday.

"Oh?" replied Aunt Martha. "And where are you going to get the money to buy them?"

Without a moment's hesitation, Jessica answered, "My daddy will give me the money."

Aunt Martha smiled as she thought of Jessica's father paying for his own birthday present. She knew that he would love his daughter for the gift, even though the money that bought it was his own. After all, Jessica didn't own a thing that her father hadn't given her. Even the gifts that her loving heart prompted her to give to him had to be paid for with his money!

How true that is of all of us in our relationship to our heavenly Father. What can we possibly give Him that wasn't His before it was ours?

"The silver is Mine and the gold is Mine," God says (Haggai 2:8). "Every animal of the forest is Mine, and the cattle on a thousand hills" (Psalm 50:10). The whole creation is the Lord's.

Indeed, we are His too! To each of us, God says, "Fear not, for I have redeemed you; I have summoned you by name; you are Mine" (Isaiah 43:1). The Bible makes it very clear that we are not our own. We were bought with a price—the blood of the Son of God Himself (1 Corinthians 6:19–20).

If all that we are and all that we have belongs to God, we can give Him nothing that is ours. We can give Him only what is His. Like Jessica, we can do no more than return God's bounty as a token of our love. And like Jessica's father, God has promised to love us for the spirit in which we give.

> We give You but Your own
> In any gifts we bring;
> All that we have is Yours alone,
> A trust from You, our king.

Held by His Hand

On a cold wintry day, a man and his little boy were walking on sidewalks covered with ice. It was the first time 3-year-old Daniel was wearing his new coat, which had deep flannel-lined pockets.

As the two approached a slippery place, the father said, "You had better let me hold your hand." But the boy's hands were snug in his pockets, and he kept them there—until he slipped and fell!

Somewhat humbled by this experience, he said, "I'll hold your hand, Daddy." He reached up and grabbed his father's hand.

Soon the two came to another slippery place. Down Daniel went again because his tiny fingers had not been able to grip his father's hand with strength.

Once more they resumed their walk, but after a moment's reflection, Daniel said with childlike confidence, "*You* hold *my* hand,

Daddy." As they went safely on their way, it was the father's hand that kept the boy from further danger.

We often have to learn that it is not our hold on God, but His hold on us that keeps our feet from slipping at the difficult spots. The Bible tells us: "[You] through faith are shielded by God's power until the coming of the salvation that is ready to be revealed" (1 Peter 1:5). It is God, not we, it is His power, not ours, that does the keeping.

As we travel the precarious path of each new day, what comfort to know that it is God's hand that will lead us and will hold us every step of the way. We know that the hand that is stretched from heaven to help us is the hand that was pierced to save us from our ruin. In His hands, we are safe. He knows us and He loves us. By the Spirit's power, we follow Him. He gives us eternal life. And no man shall pluck us from His hands (John 10:27–29).

What an appropriate prayer at the opening of each new day: "*You* hold *my* hand, Lord Jesus!"

I am trusting You, Lord Jesus,
Trusting only You;
Trusting You for full salvation,
Free and true.

I am trusting You, Lord Jesus;
Never let me fall.
I am trusting You forever
And for all.

She Got Straight As

The pastor was visiting Rachel's home. He was conducting home visits to strengthen the spiritual life of the families in his church.

After discussing spiritual matters with Rachel's parents, the pastor turned to the little girl. "Do you say your prayers every day?" the pastor asked.

"Yes, sir!" Rachel answered.

"And do you pray when you go to bed and when you get up in the morning?" the pastor asked.

"Yes, sir!" came the quick answer.

"And do you ask the Lord to bless you in your school work?" the man asked.

"No, sir! I get straight As!"

Somehow it didn't seem important to Rachel to pray for the Lord's blessing on her studies. After all, she had perfect grades!

We may smile, but let's take a serious look

at ourselves. We often become remiss in our prayers because we are getting "straight As."

When things are going wrong, when difficulties loom large on every side, when problems become unsolvable, when the deep questions of life go begging for answers, then prayer seems a very natural (yes, a very needed) exercise.

But when life becomes a succession of beautiful mornings, when it seems that "everything's going our way," when good fortune smiles on us at every turn, then prayer seems superfluous.

Prayer is never superfluous, even when we are getting "straight As." Because who is giving us those As? God, the source of all blessings. Prayer is not merely a matter of asking. It is also a matter of thanking, of praising, of communing, of confiding.

Who could ever run out of things for which to thank and praise the Lord? Or who could ever run out of things about which to speak to God?

Footprints of the Stars

My vantage point is a French window in a Hollywood hotel. I'm overlooking Hollywood Boulevard. From my room on the 12th floor, I look down at the world-famous Mann's Chinese Theater, which is just across the street.

I have looked down at this brilliantly lit Mecca of the entertainment world a hundred times before, always with a vague feeling of sadness and regret. However, I don't think I've had this feeling of poignancy before.

Day after day, year after year, morning, noon, and night, a steady parade of curious tourists lingers in front of the theater to look at the "footprints of the stars." Engraved in a vast expanse of concrete are the footprints, handprints, legprints, and autographs of well-known celebrities—many of whom are no longer among the living.

Children of all ages delight in putting their feet into the footprints so they can tell their friends back home: "I walked in the very same spot where Marilyn Monroe and Charlie Chaplin walked!"

Perhaps there is a special reason for my melancholy mood as I look down at that endless parade tonight. I have just laid aside my Bible after reading God's own tablet on which are engraved the footprints of His stars. I had read Hebrews chapter 11. "By faith, Abel; By faith, Enoch; By faith, Noah, Abraham, Isaac, Jacob, Joseph, Moses, Rahab." These are the people whose footprints God has asked us to study and to follow—the footprints of faith and love and duty.

Long after the footprints in the concrete across the street have crumbled into dust, the footprints of the faithful will continue to show the way to generations as yet unborn.

Thank God that far from the glitter and the glamour of this transitory world there is a vast unnumbered host of those who are trying, with God's help, to match their footsteps to the paths His faithful followed.

"You'll Know Where to Find Me"

An elderly pastor lay critically ill. In the opinion of his doctor, he could live only a few days more. His wife called their son, who was also a pastor and who served a congregation in a small town 300 miles away.

Within a few hours, the son was at his father's bedside. The two men prayed together.

Saturday came, and there was no change in the elderly man's condition. Calling his son to his bedside, he spoke in a weak and faltering voice: "Go back to your congregation, son, and preach tomorrow. If I should slip away while you are gone, you'll know where to find me."

"You'll know where to find me." What a wonderful thing when a father can speak like this to his children. What a wonderful thing at the sunset of life to know exactly where we will be at eternity's dawn—in our Father's house. We will be in the company of our Savior, who has gone ahead to prepare a place for us.

And what a wonderful thing for a father who is taking leave of his children to know that they, too, have learned the way to the place where he is going. He can rest securely because they, too, by God's grace, will share a mansion in the Father's house above.

Those of us who are parents should consider whether we have arrived at that spiritual certainty that will enable us, at the end of life, to say, "I know where I am going." Then we can ask ourselves if we have passed on this knowledge and this faith to our children so we can say confidently to them, "You'll know where to find me."

We can do both if, by God's grace, our faith and that of our children is rooted firmly in Him who died for us and who even now is awaiting our arrival in His Father's house above.

Too Poor to Pay

In a Scottish village lived a doctor noted for his generosity. After his death, when his books were examined, quite a few of his accounts were found to have a line written across them in red ink: "Forgiven. Too poor to pay."

Some months after his death, his widow insisted that these bills must be paid. She immediately initiated court proceedings.

After examining one bill after another, the lawyer asked the widow, "Is this your husband's handwriting in red?" She admitted that it was.

"Then," said the lawyer, "there is no court in the land that can obtain the money for you. If your husband has written *forgiven*, these debts are forgiven."

God has written *forgiven* over the record of sin of those who believe in Christ as Savior. The Bible says: "God was reconciling the world to Himself in Christ, not counting men's sins against them" (2 Corinthians 5:19). It also says, "He forgave us all our sins, having canceled the written code, … that was against us … nailing it to the cross" (Colossians 2:13–14).

Indeed, that is the central purpose of the entire Bible: to tell us that when Christ died on the cross for our sins, His Father wrote *forgiven* across our guilty record. Our conscience, our human reason, and the unbelieving world may challenge that assertion. They may do their best to convince us that the debt of our iniquity has not been canceled.

But we have the word of God, to whom the debt was owed and who alone has the power to forgive. He has written His assurance in crimson letters: "In [Jesus] we have redemption through His blood, the forgiveness of sins, in accordance with the riches of God's grace" (Ephesians 1:7).

The eternal Son of God Himself paid for those who because of their spiritual poverty were "too poor to pay."

"Lucky Boy!"

A few Christmases ago, a distressed mother who could no longer care for her infant son gave him to a state agency for adoption. Little did she or anyone else know that within a few weeks the child would be adopted by a wealthy couple in California—a couple whose annual income is in the millions.

After all requirements had been met and all the necessary documents had been signed, the 15-month-old was declared the legal heir of a fortune that came close to $20 million.

We might say, "Lucky boy!" upon hearing this story. At least, we hope that his sudden change of social status proves to be a blessing.

What this wealthy couple did for this infant at Christmas, God did for us on the very first Christmas—only in a much higher sense. Through the miracle of Christmas, God made it possible for us to be adopted into His family and to be made heirs of eternal, indescribable, and immeasurable treasures.

The Bible tells us that by nature we were not God's children. Instead, we were "gratifying the cravings of our sinful nature" (Ephesians 2:3). It also tells us that on the first Christmas, "when the time had fully come, God sent His Son, born of a woman, born under law, to redeem those under law, that we might receive the full rights of sons. So you are no longer a slave, but a son; and since you are a son, God has made you also an heir" (Galatians 4:4–5, 7).

Because of what happened on that first Christmas, we are sons and daughters of God. Heirs of God through Christ—that is the message of Christmas. Having been adopted into the family of God, we have come into possession of the treasures of heaven: forgiveness of sins; fellowship with God; full, free, abundant, and eternal life.

Because Christ became a Son of earth, we are children of heaven.

> We are rich, for He was poor;
> Is not this a wonder?
> Therefore praise God evermore
> Here on earth and yonder.

She Wasn't Lost

A father and his 6-year-old daughter were walking through the downtown streets of the city to which they recently had moved. With almost no conversation between them, they turned corner after corner, taking in the sights of the unfamiliar streets.

After some time, the little girl asked, "Daddy, are you lost?" There was an anxious look on her face, which did not escape her father. Instead of answering her directly, he tightened his grip on her hand and asked, "Are you lost?"

A smile brightened her face. "Oh, no" she said quickly. "I'm with you, Daddy!" With that her fears were gone.

How could this little girl be lost as long as she was with her father? or as long as he was with her? How can you and I be lost as long as we know that our heavenly Father is with us and we are with Him?

As we turn the corner of each new day, each new week, or each new year and look down the long and unfamiliar road that lies ahead, we may shrink from the uninviting prospect. There are so many uncertainties, so many problems, so many pitfalls, so many dangers.

Sometimes as we stand falteringly in the present and look trembling into the future, we feel that we are lost and alone in an unfriendly world. We feel unequal to the task of carrying on. Sometimes we feel lost in a world that is upside down, topsy-turvy.

As we stand at each new turn on the pathway of life, we can remember that our heavenly Father is never lost. We who have become His children through faith in Jesus Christ are forever safe within His keeping.

With our hands in His, we can walk courageously into today and into the many tomorrows that still lie before us. Each tomorrow belongs to Him.

What God Looks Like

It happened during vacation Bible school. The first-grade children were asked to draw a picture of anything or anyone they chose. After a minute or two, Hannah looked over the shoulder of Peter. "What are you going to draw?" she asked.

"I'm drawing a picture of God," Peter said.

Assuming an air of superior wisdom, Hannah retorted, "But nobody knows what God looks like!"

Peter replied with sudden determination, "They will when I'm through."

I don't know what Peter finally put on his paper, but I like the feeling behind the attempt. He was determined that when he was through, the other children would have a better idea of what God is like.

Isn't that the purpose of every Christian life—to show the people around us what God is like? St. Paul says that we are the epistles of

Christ, "written not with ink but with the Spirit of the living God, not on tablets of stone but on tablets of human hearts" (2 Corinthians 3:3).

One of the chief purposes of our being in this world is to show people through word and deed what God is like. We are to communicate the vital facts of divine revelation: that God is holy, just, and righteous but also merciful, kind, and gracious through Jesus Christ, His Son.

We may not have Peter's pencil in our hand, but we do have a life in our hands. And with that life, we can show the world "what God is like."

A Star in God's Window

It was an early spring evening during World War I. A father and his 4-year-old son were taking a leisurely stroll through a residential neighborhood. As they walked by a darkened home, Charles noticed a service flag in the window. It had a gold star on a field of white.

"What kind of flag is that, Daddy?" Charles asked.

"That star means that the people in that home have lost a son in the war. Their boy died fighting for our freedom," the father explained.

His question answered, Charles was satisfied. Quietly he walked by his father's side as they continued down the street.

A few moments later, a twinkling star appeared in the sky over the chimney of a house almost a block away. It was the first star of the evening, and it caught the attention of the boy.

As if struck by a new and momentous thought, the boy asked, "Daddy, did God lose a son in the war?"

Momentarily at a loss for words, the father looked down at his son, laid a hand on his head, and smiled. "Yes, Charles. God did give up His Son. His Son died on a cross so you and I and Mom and all people might be free.

"I pray that as long as you live," the father continued, "every time you see a star in the window of the sky, you will think of God's Son and what He did for us."

His question answered, Charles was satisfied again. He walked quietly by his father's side as they continued toward home.

As the older man looked at the golden star shimmering in the distance, he thought to himself: "For God so loved the world that He gave His one and only Son, that whoever believes in Him shall not perish but have eternal life" (John 3:16).

"But I'm Your Father!"

The son of a wealthy and respected citizen was convicted of a serious offense. Not only did the man's behavior bring disgrace to the family, but it involved the family in a lawsuit that threatened its fortune.

The young man was worried about how his father would react. Would his father turn on him in fury and berate him for his horrible act?

When the remorseful young man finally met his father, the older man did nothing of the sort. "Son," he said, "I do not condone the terrible things you have done. I condemn them with every fiber of my being. But I'm your father. I'm determined to suffer with you."

In a similar but immeasurably higher sense, God took pity on His erring sons and daughters. He condemned their transgressions, and He loathed their sins. But in His mercy, He determined to identify Himself with the sufferings that resulted from their wickedness.

God decided to suffer not only with His wayward children, but *for* them. That is the central message of the Gospel. "But God demonstrates His own love for us in this: While we were still sinners, Christ died for us" (Romans 5:8).

Who showed His love toward us? God! Who died for us? Christ! There may be much mystery tied up in that sentence, but there can be no doubt about its message: The God of heaven took pity on His erring children and, through Jesus Christ, His Son, He suffered in their stead.

God entered into human suffering through His own beloved Son so He could "see us through," so our penalty could be paid, so we could be free forever. The Scriptures say of Christ: "He was pierced for our transgressions … by His wounds we are healed" (Isaiah 53:5).

God did not have to do this for us. But God is our Father, so He did.

My Sermons—
Where Are They?

The pastor and his wife were working in his study, packing books and papers, preparing to move into the new parsonage.

Since he had entered the ministry, the pastor had saved manuscripts of his sermons in separate bundles, one for each year. An index card on which was written the year identified each package.

In his hands, the pastor held sermons for the last three years, but he couldn't find the sermons for the current year. He asked his wife in a worried tone, "Where are this year's sermons?"

Half humorously, half philosophically, his wife replied, "I've often wondered!"

She had often wondered what became of a sermon after it was preached. She didn't doubt the effective power of the Gospel, but in her weaker moments, she had her misgivings about the permanent effect of many of her husband's sermons.

Perhaps we all have wondered what has become of a sermon we heard. It's like asking what happened to yesterday's sunshine. In one sense, it is gone. In another sense, it is here. It has gone into grains and fruits and vegetables that will sustain life. In the food we eat, the sunshine of yesterday is carrying out God's purposes.

Where are the already-preached sermons? They have come and gone, but by God's grace, they accomplished and continue to accomplish His purposes.

God Himself has said, "So is My word... . It will not return to Me empty, but will accomplish what I desire and achieve the purpose for which I sent it" (Isaiah 55:11).

That applies not only to this year's sermons, but to all those we have ever heard.

The Congregation Was Perfectly Behaved

The church service was one of the most orderly I had ever attended. The worshipers sat in their pews erect, wide awake, and alert.

They eagerly participated in every part of the service. They sang each hymn with fervor, spoke each prayer precisely and with conviction. When the preacher announced his text, every eye in the assembly was riveted on the man who was about to bring a message from God's Word.

There was no squirming in the pews, no whispered conversation, no yawning, no searching of purses for chewing gum or cough drops, no craning of necks, no looking back to see if Aunt Jane or Uncle Jim were sitting in the balcony.

In fact, if I had not known the reason for this almost perfect decorum, I would not have believed my eyes or ears. But I knew the reason!

In the back of the church, as well as in the

balcony and in the far corners of the building, were television cameras. At strategic points throughout the sanctuary there were well-concealed microphones.

These electronic eyes and ears were trained on every worshiper (at least, so it seemed), recording every act and preserving it permanently. Just hours later, the entire worship service would be shown to countless television viewers.

With these almost omnipresent eyes and ears, every worshiper was on his or her best behavior. I couldn't help but think how different the average worship service would be if each of us were as keenly aware of the invisible eye and ear of the Almighty, which are present every Sunday morning!

"You are the God who sees me" (Genesis 16:13). God sees our every act and hears our every thought.

None of Our Business?

It happened during the Great Depression. A mother and her 4-year-old daughter were walking along a downtown street when they saw a shabbily dressed man. He was standing at a corner, holding out his ragged cap, and asking for a few pennies.

"Oh Mama," said the girl as she tugged on her mother's coat sleeve, "let's help him."

The mother reached for her daughter's hand and hurried her along. "Come along, dear. It isn't any of our business," she said.

Not quite sure that she had understood her mother, the little girl still obeyed. Before long she forgot about the man at the corner as her mind became occupied with the items in the store windows.

That night during her bedtime prayers, the girl said in childlike innocence, "Please God, bless that poor man on the corner." After saying *amen,* she met her mother's eyes. Then she remembered what her mother had said that afternoon. She quickly folded her hands again and said, "Oh, no, God. He really isn't any of our business, is he?"

We don't know what the mother thought or said, but she may have spoken to God herself later.

Yes, the poor of this world are God's business. They are our business too. The millions of people all over the world who are ill-fed, ill-clad, ill-housed—the refugees, the displaced, the helpless, and the hopeless—all of them are God's business and ours.

The Lord admonishes His people: "Let us not become weary in doing good, for at the proper time we will reap a harvest if we do not give up. Therefore, as we have opportunity, let us do good to all people, especially to those who belong to the family of believers" (Galatians 6:9–10).

When the Signs Got Mixed

The suburban residents of a Midwest town were half amused, half confused, when they approached an intersection one morning and found more than a dozen traffic signs. Each one gave a contradictory direction.

They learned later that a traffic crew had deposited the signs at the corner temporarily, awaiting the arrival of another truck to carry them to their proper destination.

Meanwhile the miscellaneous assortment of signs shouted to all approaching motorists: "No Left Turn"; "Turn Left"; "Stop"; "Turn Right."

Not so amusing, but infinitely more confusing, is the plight of many people today who are looking for the "right road" to salvation. With more than 200 brands of religion in the United States alone, they don't know which "sign" to follow.

Amid this confusion of directions, there is a

"sign" that we can follow with absolute assurance. Our Savior says: "I am the way and the truth and the life. No one comes to the Father except through Me" (John 14:6).

The one and only road that leads to heaven, according to the Bible, is Jesus our Savior. "Salvation is found in no one else, for there is no other name under heaven given to men by which we must be saved" (Acts 4:12).

The road to heaven always leads across Mount Calvary. Any sign that promises heaven by a different road is false.

When the Lights Go Out

It was a late autumn evening during World War II. The entire city of London lay in inky darkness because of a strictly enforced blackout.

After the evening meal was over, a London father invited his 8-year-old son to take a walk with him. As they walked down the darkened streets, the boy remarked, "Daddy, we never saw the stars over the city until the lights went out."

How true! True not only of the dark nights over London, but true also of the dark nights that again and again settle over our lives. How often have we had good reason to lift our eyes heavenward and exclaim: "O Father, I never saw Your stars over my life until the lights went out!"

Sometimes it takes the darkness of sadness or sickness, loneliness or bereavement, disappointment or disillusionment, anxiety or despair to bring out the radiance and the brilliance of God's firmament of Gospel promises.

How often in the silent darkness of some depressing sorrow have we been cheered by the warm light of those promises, shimmering like stars in the heavens: "I am with you always" (Matthew 28:20). "Do not be afraid, for I am with you" (Genesis 26:24). "I will never leave you nor forsake you" (Joshua 1:5).

In the broad daylight when everything is going our way, when health, wealth, and happy friendships cheer us, our eyes sometimes lose sight of these promises. But when the lights are out, when health and wealth and friends are gone, these promises are still there, eternal in the Gospel firmament. People and fortunes may change, but God's assurances go on forever. They are like the stars in His heavens.

Whether the lights of our life are on or off, may our eyes be fixed on God's unchanging Gospel. It is there—in darkness and in light.

Taller Than Before

A traveling salesman was chatting with an eccentric farmer whom he hoped to interest in some new farm equipment.

Seated on the porch with his not-too-promising prospect, the salesman noticed a rough drawing of what looked like a barn lying on a nearby chair.

Picking it up and studying it for a moment, he asked the farmer if this were a drawing of a new barn he intended to build.

"Yep," replied the farmer.

Puzzled, the salesman inquired, "Why is it so wide and so long and only about half as tall as a normal barn?"

The farmer had his own reasons for drawing his plan, but being in no mood to prolong this boring conversation, he replied, "So when it gets blown over, it'll be higher than it was before."

We may not fully appreciate the farmer's

sense of humor, but we can extract some wisdom from his reply. It's important to plan our life "so when it gets blown over, it will be higher than it was before."

Lives are built that way if they are built on the sure foundation of Christ, if their roots are sunk deep into the immovable assurances that God has given us in His Son.

The pages of history are filled with the triumphs of Christians whose lives were blown topsy-turvy by the winds of adversity but who went on to splendid achievements despite the very winds that seemed to spell calamity. God made their lives taller because they had been blown over!

Do our lives stand firm on the immovable foundation of God, the foundation He has provided in Christ?

"Mother, Are You Worrying?"

"Mother, are you worrying?"

Mrs. Carter was startled by this unexpected question. Standing in the doorway to the living room was 5-year-old Philip. He was in his pajamas and looked as though he hadn't a friend in the world.

Mrs. Carter had put her son to bed more than an hour ago and thought that he had long since drifted off to sleep. But there he was in the doorway, wide awake and evidently troubled.

At a loss to explain what Philip meant by his unusual query, she soon found out what was troubling him. When she had put him to bed, he had confided to her a problem that had to be solved by the next morning.

In true mother fashion, Mrs. Carter had assured Philip that everything would be all right. As she tucked him in and kissed him good night, she had said, "Now, you just go to sleep and let me worry about that."

An hour had passed and Philip wasn't sure that his mother was keeping her promise. Was she really worrying about his problem? Maybe she had forgotten? He had to make sure. So he crawled out of bed, crept down the stairs, peeked into the living room, and asked, "Mother, are you worrying?"

We may smile at Philip's predicament, but we are a lot like him. The Bible invites us again and again to cast all our cares, all our worries, and all our anxieties on the Lord. He assures us that He will care for us (1 Peter 5:7).

Because we are spiritual children, we find it difficult to take God at His word. We often stay awake at night because we aren't sure God will keep His promise to care for us. But God's "good night" to the Christian is similar to that of Philip's mother: "You go to sleep and let Me worry about that."

If You Want to See
the Christ Child

Christmas 1906 was going to be a cheerless day for the Ericksens. In poor health and out of work, Lars had reached the point where he didn't care if Christmas ever came or not. Depressed and irritable, he made poor company for his wife, Anna, and his 5-year-old daughter, Greta.

On this particular evening, Greta was busily at work with her scissors, cardboard, and glue. She was constructing a crude Nativity, which she had spread out on the floor in front of the coal stove.

"How do you like it, Daddy?" she asked.

"Fine," he answered disinterestedly.

"How do you like the manger?" Greta asked.

"I can't see it from here," was his grumpy reply.

Looking at her daddy, Greta said, "If you want to see the Christ Child, you'll have to get down on your knees."

How true! True not only of Lars Ericksen, but also of us. If we want to see the Christ Child, we'll have to get down on our knees. If there were a special Beatitude for Christmas, it would be: "Blessed are the poor in spirit for they will see the Infant Christ."

Blessed are they who come to the manger meek and lowly. They will see the "Wonderful Counselor, Mighty God, Everlasting Father, Prince of Peace" (Isaiah 9:6).

As we travel in spirit to Bethlehem's manger, we can approach the Christ Child in true humility. If we bring Him our weakness, He will give us strength. If we bring Him our sorrows, He will give us joy. Above all, if we bring Him our sins, He will give us full and free pardon.

So "if you want to see the Christ Child, you will have to get down on your knees."

The Clock That Stopped

A clock in a jeweler's window stopped one day for only half an hour. The hands stood still at twenty minutes after eight.

Children on their way to school, noticing the time, stopped to play. People on their way to work, when they saw the clock, slowed their pace. A man hurrying to catch a train slackened his gait when he saw that he still had plenty of time.

The children were late for school, the adults were late for work, and the man missed his train—all because one clock had stopped! Never had these people realized how much they had depended on that clock, until the first time it had led them astray.

Everyone who professes the Christian faith is like that clock. People all around us are, consciously or unconsciously, influenced by what we say and do.

If our Christianity "stops" for just a little

while, if careless speech or improper conduct sets a bad example, we may lead others astray. It is wrong to assume that our lives, just because they appear insignificant, do not count; that our actions are unimportant; that our influence is insignificant. God has placed every Christian into the world to "tell the time," to influence others as we journey toward eternity.

"You are the light of the world," says Christ (Matthew 5:14). You are an instrument in God's hands to bring others to Him and to heaven. How important, then, that those who read our lives be led into paths of truth.

A stopped clock tells the truth only twice a day. All the rest of its life is a lie! God has no use for "stopped clocks" in His kingdom.

A Debt of Love

A soldier in the South Pacific lay unconscious for days in an improvised hospital behind the lines. He was critically in need of blood, but there was no plasma to be had. A sergeant with whom he had not been on friendly terms volunteered to give some of his own blood to save the life of the young soldier.

When the wounded man returned to consciousness a few days later, he was told that he owed his life to the sergeant whom he had previously regarded with disdain. He wanted to thank his benefactor, but the sergeant had been transferred to another island that morning. It was not at all certain that the two men would ever meet again.

"I'll find him, if it's the last thing I do," said the young soldier. "I owe my life to him, and I won't rest until I thank him!"

The way that soldier felt toward the man whose blood had spelled the difference between life and death is the way we feel toward Jesus Christ. "I owe my life to Him, and I won't rest until I thank Him!"

A divine restlessness seizes the hearts of those who are keenly aware of the price of redemption. We cannot be at ease until we have poured out the last full measure of devotion to Christ, who has redeemed our souls from death.

The Christian life is the response of gratitude to the Redeemer expressed by the redeemed. Every deed of love, every kindness, every conscious act of Christian virtue is a thank-You to the one who paid the price of our salvation.

The apostle Paul put it eloquently when he wrote to the Galatians: "I have been crucified with Christ and I no longer live, but Christ lives in me. The life I live in the body, I live by faith in the Son of God, who loved me and gave Himself for me" (Galatians 2:20).

Paul could have voiced his devotion to Christ in the words of the young soldier: "I owe my life to Him, and I won't rest until I thank Him." Do we say the same?

He Rose Again!

A well-dressed gentleman was standing in front of the display window of an art gallery. He was looking at a painting of the crucifixion.

As he stood there, a little boy in dirty blue jeans and a tattered sweatshirt walked up and stood beside him. He also stared at the painting.

Pointing to the picture, the man asked the boy: "Do you know who that is hanging on the cross?"

"Yes, sir," came the quick response. "That's the Savior."

As he spoke, the boy's eyes showed surprise and pity at the ignorance of the unknown gentleman. Then, after a pause and with an evident desire to enlighten the man, the boy added, "Those are the soldiers, the Roman soldiers. And that lady crying is His mother."

After another brief moment of silence, the boy added, "They killed Him, mister. They killed Him."

Together the man and the boy studied the painting in silence. Finally the man tousled the boy's hair and walked away, disappearing into the crowd.

He had turned a corner and walked a half-block when suddenly he heard the shrill voice of the boy. He was calling "Hey, mister!" as he made his way through the crowd.

The man turned and waited for the youngster to catch up with him. Almost out of breath, the boy panted his excited information: "I wanted to tell you: He rose again! He rose again!"

What a message!

Whether the boy realized it or not, he would never again in all his life deliver a message of greater importance. Nothing would ever provide a more important headline than the one his youthful lips had just formed: "He rose again!"

God's greatest message to us is the message of His Son. It may be formed on the lips of a child: "They killed Him. He rose again." Or it may be recorded in His Book: "He was delivered over to death for our sins and was raised to life for our justification" (Romans 4:25).

Unforgivable?

A distressed mother came to her pastor with the confession: "Pastor, I have committed the unpardonable sin."

The clergyman gave no sign of surprise or alarm but asked her in a restrained and quiet voice, "Are you sorry for it?"

"Yes, Pastor, dreadfully sorry," was her anguished reply.

"Then you have committed nothing that cannot be forgiven," said the pastor. "There is no sin, no matter how great, that cannot be forgiven through sincere repentance and trusting faith in Jesus, our Redeemer."

Behind that simple, reassuring answer lay the full authority of Scripture. It was not the pastor speaking, but God speaking through him to the woman's troubled conscience.

That is the supreme glory and comfort of the Gospel. The disease cannot spread farther than the cure. "Where sin increased, grace increased all the more" (Romans 5:20).

There was sufficient grace for penitent Peter, who "went outside and wept bitterly" (Matthew 26:75). There was sufficient grace for anguished Paul, who cried out: "What a wretched man I am!" (Romans 7:24). There was sufficient grace for the sin-burdened tax collector, who beat his breast and said, "God, have mercy on me, a sinner" (Luke 18:13).

There is sufficient grace for you! All who have learned to look with terror at their own sins and have learned to lift pleading eyes toward Calvary's cross for the assurance of forgiveness have found a limitless reservoir of divine grace.

No matter who you are, no matter how far you have drifted from God and His Word, no matter how great your sin, the Savior's promise is still for you: "Whoever comes to Me I will never drive away" (John 6:37).

> I heard the voice of Jesus say,
> "Come unto Me and rest;
> Lay down, O weary one, lay down
> Your head upon My breast."
> I came to Jesus as I was
> So weary, worn, and sad;
> I found in Him a resting place,
> And He has made me glad.

Familiar Darkness

Three-year-old Michelle was spending the weekend with her aunt and uncle. It was the first time she had ever been away from her dad and mom overnight.

She had played all day and had enjoyed every minute. Her aunt had just read her a bedtime story, had listened to her prayers, tucked her snugly in bed, and kissed her good night. As she left the room, she whispered "sleep tight" and turned out the light.

Sometime later, she passed the child's room again and thought she heard restrained sobbing. Opening the bedroom door, she found Michelle crying her heart out. "What is it, Michelle?" she asked.

"I'm afraid in the dark," the child cried.

"But you always sleep in the dark at home," her aunt tried to assure her.

"Yes. But that's *my* dark," Michelle sobbed.

Her "dark" was different. The "dark" in her

room held no terror because she knew what was in her room in the light: her doll, her teddy bear, her rocking chair, her toy chest. Michelle knew where each one was in the light, and she knew that they must still be there in the dark, surrounding her at night just as they surrounded her during the day. So she was not afraid in *her* dark!

What a striking picture of the believing child of God. We live through the night of our own adversity, the night of our own sorrow, trial, and affliction. But having looked into the face of Christ, we are not afraid of "our dark" because amid that "dark," we are aware of the comforting presence of Christ, whom our eye of faith has seen in darkness and in light.

We know that Christ is with us in our "dark," even as He has been with us in our light. He reaches out His hand to ours, speaking pardon to our souls, whispering assurance to our hearts.

In darkness and in light, He has assured us: "Never will I leave you, never will I forsake you" (Hebrews 13:5). Darkness and light are both alike to Him.

A Sermon on a Bus

It was a blazing-hot day in St. Louis. The temperature was in the high 90s. I was standing on a downtown corner, bathed in perspiration, waiting for an air-conditioned bus.

Suddenly it turned the corner and stopped in front of me. I lost no time in boarding. As I stepped out of the scorching sun into the refrigerated vehicle, I was shocked by the sudden change in temperature.

For a block or two, I sat miserably uncomfortable, my body quivering, my teeth chattering. I debated whether to leave the bus. Would I be able to stand this for the 40-minute ride? Would I catch a cold?

Eyeing the other passengers, I chided myself for such cowardly thoughts and began reading my magazine. Soon I was absorbed in its contents.

Perhaps 10 minutes later, I laid the magazine aside and began to reflect. Why was I suddenly so comfortable? What had become of the icy air? When had the change taken place? And what had actually changed—the temperature in the bus or I?

The temperature in the bus hadn't changed! It was I. Without being aware of it, I had become comfortable in the atmosphere that only 10 minutes earlier had seemed so shocking. The air in the bus hadn't changed; I had.

What a parable of life. Imperceptibly, the atmosphere of the world closes in on us! Gradually we become acclimated to the allurements of worldly pleasure. Unconsciously we lose our sense of shock.

Many Christians who previously would have shuddered at the thought or at the sight of certain sins now find themselves completely comfortable in their presence. To them it may seem that these sins have changed. These sins seem to have become less sinful in God's sight. But it is not the sins that have changed; it is the sinner.

We have every reason to ask the Holy Spirit to keep us on our guard so we will not become comfortable when God would have us be shocked.

Limping
at the Shepherd's Side

A traveler in Palestine joined a shepherd as he led his flock across a hill. As they walked and conversed, the traveler noticed one sheep that walked with some difficulty. It stayed within a short distance of the shepherd.

Curious, he asked the shepherd why this sheep walked with a noticeable limp and why it never ventured more than a few feet away.

"That sheep is one of the oldest in the flock," explained the shepherd. "Soon after it was born, I learned that it was partially deaf. When it was a little lamb, it persisted in straying from the fold where it could not hear my voice.

"Many times I had to rescue it from death," he continued. "Finally, I had to inflict that injury on its leg myself. Ever since that day, the sheep has limped, but it also has stayed much closer to me for guidance and protection."

The apostle Paul had a similar "limp." He

called it his thorn in the flesh. To him it was "a messenger of Satan to torment me. Three times I pleaded with the Lord to take it away from me. But He said to me: 'My grace is sufficient for you, for My power is made perfect in weakness' " (2 Corinthians 12:7–9).

If God has given us a burden that is causing us to limp, we can trust that He wants to use that burden to draw us closer to His side.

"Of His Kingdom
There Shall Be No End"

E. Stanley Jones tells how he once traveled from France to India by plane. In the early morning, he left Marseilles and stopped to refuel at Corsica. He remembered that it was from this island that Napoleon had set off to conquer the world.

At noon, Jones lunched in Naples. As he ate, his mind went back to the Caesars, who had set off from this land to subdue the earth.

At nightfall, Jones was in Greece. He thought about Alexander the Great, who started from this ancient land to be a world conqueror.

The next day, he flew over Assyria and Babylon, lands from which mighty monarchs had gone forth to make the earth tremble.

As Jones flew over these countries, he was struck by the fact that every one of these mighty empires and powerful dictators is dead and gone. Within each empire had been the seed of its own decay and dissolution—the seed of human sin.

Only one empire that began in the lands over which Jones flew still remains. That is the empire that began humbly in the unspectacular land of Palestine, in the little town of Bethlehem.

The King who was born in a stable, cradled in straw, rejected by men, and nailed to a cross still reigns! He reigns in heaven among His holy angels. He reigns in His church, which He rules by love and someday will bring victorious to His homeland. He reigns on earth by the might of His omnipotence, still governing the destinies of nations.

Napoleons, Caesars, and Alexanders have come and gone. Dictators, despots, conquerors still march across the pages of history. Each has his day.

But of the Babe who was born in Bethlehem, God Himself has told us: "He will be great and will be called the Son of the Most High. ... His kingdom will never end" (Luke 1:32–33).

Small wonder that from millions of hearts

and voices and from unnumbered "kindreds and tongues and people and nations" there still comes the age-old call:

Oh, come, let us adore Him,
Christ the Lord!

God's Broken Heart

An unbeliever was seated in the pastor's study. Although he was a sincere seeker after truth, he nevertheless found it impossible to reconcile all the wickedness and misery in the world with the Bible's doctrine of the goodness and the mercy of God.

"If God were really good, all of the misery and wickedness in the world would break His heart," he said.

"It did," replied the pastor. Then he pointed to a painting of the crucifixion on the far wall of his study.

Have you ever thought of the crucifixion as the breaking of God's heart because of the sinfulness and stubbornness of His rebellious creatures? Have you thought of it as the breaking of God's heart because of your shameful record of disobedience and sin?

In a very real sense the story of the suffering and death of Jesus Christ, our Lord, is the story of the breaking heart of God. It was breaking because of the world's iniquity.

The Scriptures tell us that God loved the world so much that He willingly surrendered, sacrificed, gave up, His only begotten Son. He sent Jesus to suffer and to die in the place of fallen sinners.

The Scriptures tell us that this Son, who lived with His Father in the heavens, "was despised and rejected by men, a man of sorrows, and familiar with suffering. ... But He was pierced for our transgressions, He was crushed for our iniquities; the punishment that brought us peace was upon Him, and by His wounds we are healed" (Isaiah 53:3, 5).

In a preeminent sense it is true that when cruel hands nailed our Savior to His cross, God was there! God was there, fashioning the salvation of a world of misery and wickedness. For "God was reconciling the world to Himself in Christ, not counting men's sins against them. ... God made Him who had no sin to be sin for us, so that in Him we might become the righteousness of God" (2 Corinthians 5:19, 21).

Yes, on that first Good Friday the heart of God did break for your sins and for mine. And we can bring Him our broken hearts, broken in contrition and repentance, in return.

My Father Understands

Amy had spilled some paint on the back porch. She had tried not to, but she had!

"What will your father say?" asked her friend, Erin.

"He'll understand," was Amy's confident reply.

Amy was right. Her father did understand and willingly forgave her. After all, who understands us better than our father or our mother? Who is more ready to forgive us when we fail, or to cover our shortcomings with the mantle of love?

The parent's heart remembers the limitations of the child. In that remembrance, the parent is moved to love and pity.

It's the same for our heavenly Father. The psalmist writes:

He does not treat us as our sins deserve
or repay us according to our iniquities.

For as high as the heavens are above
the earth, so great is His love for those
who fear Him; as far as the east is from
the west, so far has He removed our
transgressions from us. As a father has
compassion on his children, so the LORD
has compassion on those who fear Him;
for He knows how we are formed,
He remembers that we are dust.
Psalm 103:10–14

"He knows how we are formed"—that we are so weak, so erring, so sinful. That is why God offers us a salvation that is full and free, not dependent on our own merit.

In Christ and His atoning work, we have everything that the loving heart of God could give: forgiveness of sins today and every day and eternal life with God in the everlasting mansions.

What peace, what joy, what confidence we have to know that in heaven we have a Father who understands, who knows us by name, and who, knowing us, forgives us!

Our Proof of Life Eternal

People down through the ages have sought proof of life beyond the grave. In our day, it has become fashionable to point to the dying leaves of autumn and to the tender shoots of springtime as pictures of human death and resurrection—and as pledges of life beyond the tomb.

But when the cold fingers of icy death come tapping on our shoulder, there will be no comfort in the fact that October is the time of falling leaves and springtime is the season when lilacs and lilies bloom! At that moment, nothing less will comfort our turbulent souls than the vision of our Savior, triumphant in the skies, with the seal of victory over death in His nail-pierced hands. From His lips will come the assurance: "Because I live, you also will live" (John 14:19).

Christ's victory over the grave is our proof of life eternal. His empty tomb proclaims to us that someday our grave, too, will be empty.

"Christ ... the firstfruits of those who have fallen asleep," says Paul (1 Corinthians 15:20). Just as the firstfruits are the foretaste, the proof, of a later harvest, so Christ's resurrection is the guarantee and proof of our resurrection to life eternal in that later harvest.

For us, death holds no terror. Our mighty Champion has gone before us through the valley of the shadow. He has prepared the way so we can follow. He has lifted the cloud that hung heavily over what seemed to be the journey's end. Now we can see that at the end of the road that winds up the far side of the valley is our Father's house with all its many mansions.

Christ's glorious resurrection on that first Easter morning is our proof of life eternal.

> He lives and grants me daily breath;
> He lives, and I shall conquer death;
> He lives my mansion to prepare;
> He lives to bring me safely there.

Are We Getting Ready?

Justin came home from Sunday school and said to his mother: "Mama, my teacher told us that God puts people into this world so they can get ready for heaven."

Almost without thinking, his mother replied, "Yes, dear, that's right."

Wrinkling his forehead into a thoughtful frown, Justin hesitated a moment, then asked, "Then why don't we see anybody getting ready?"

A childlike question, yet how true! If God puts people into this world so they can get ready for heaven, why don't we see anybody getting ready?

In the hurry and hubbub of our busy world, people have become so preoccupied with the affairs of the day, with the pressing problems of this world, that many have forgotten all about "getting ready" for the next world. Yet the psalmist tells us: "You sweep men away in the sleep of death; they are like the new grass of the morning—though in the morning it springs up new, by evening it is dry and withered" (Psalm 90:5–6).

We have every reason to continue with the psalmist and pray: "Teach us to number our days aright, that we may gain a heart of wisdom" (Psalm 90:12). In other words, we ask God to teach us to "get ready." We ask Him to teach us to regard this life as a period of preparation for a greater and more wonderful life. This new life will be with God and all the redeemed in heaven. We ask God to teach us to use our days and our years so they stretch toward our heavenly home.

Are we really "getting ready"? Do we daily confess our sins to God and ask Him in Jesus' name to forgive us? Does our entire case, for time and for eternity, rest in the hands of Jesus, who is able to save all those who believe in Him? Then in the words of Justin, we are ready.

He Knew the Shepherd

It happened many years ago. A group of well-educated people were gathered at the home of a friend for a sociable evening. Among them was a popular actor of the day.

During the course of the evening, the actor was asked to give a reading. He obliged by reading the Twenty-third Psalm. Everyone was impressed by his deep, rich voice, his clear enunciation, and the rhythmic rise and fall of his well-measured tones. He was an artist!

After he had finished, the group asked an older clergyman to present the same material. He declined, but he asked permission to explain certain verses from an historical and geographical perspective and in the light of their New Testament fulfillment in Jesus, the Good Shepherd.

As the clergyman expounded on the beautiful psalm, he became more and more absorbed in his message, completely forgetting himself in the process. At the end, almost involuntarily, he quoted the entire psalm as the humble confession of his believing heart. Particularly moving was the confidence with which he repeated the words: "Yea, though I walk through the valley of the shadow of death, I will fear no evil; for Thou art with me; Thy rod and Thy staff they comfort me."

The light of faith shone in his eyes as he concluded, "Surely goodness and mercy shall follow me all the days of my life: and I will dwell in the house of the LORD for ever."

A hush fell over the group as the older clergyman sat down. There had been a difference in the two readings. But the question was how to define the difference. Later that evening, one of the guests put his finger on the difference: "The actor knew the Shepherd's Psalm, but the pastor knew the Shepherd."

More to Follow

The story is told of a well-to-do man who died and left detailed instructions regarding the disposition of his wealth. Among other things, a certain sum was designated for a minister who had frequently served the family.

The widow decided to give the money to the minister in regular installments. She mailed him $100 and placed a slip of paper inside the envelope. The paper read, "More to follow."

Every two weeks, without fail, the clergyman would find the identical amount of money in his mailbox with the identical message: "More to follow."

More to follow! That is Christ's unbreakable pledge to all who believe in Him. The blessings that we receive today are only a pledge of those we will receive tomorrow. Those we receive tomorrow will bear the pledge of heaven: "More to follow." God's mercies are new every morning. His compassions never fail.

The evangelist John, in his gospel, speaks of the inexhaustible riches of Christ and says: "From the fullness of His grace we have all received one blessing after another" (John 1:16). One version says, "grace upon grace." Christ's goodness pours in on us like the waves of the sea. As one pours over us, there is always another close behind, and another and another. Christ's capacity and willingness to supply our needs, both spiritual and material, are unlimited and eternal.

There is no need in our life, however great or small, that Christ does not know and which He will not fill, if it is necessary for our eternal welfare. "My God will meet all your needs according to His glorious riches in Christ Jesus," says Paul (Philippians 4:19).

We who have such a bountiful Savior need never fear that His grace and goodness might run out. From His hand we have received, and we shall continue to receive, "grace upon grace." From His inexhaustible spiritual resources, there will always be "more to follow."

Sand in My Shoe!

A man who had hitchhiked from coast to coast, and who had walked many miles in the process, was asked what was most difficult to endure.

To the surprise of his questioner, it was not the steep mountains or the dazzling sun or the scorching desert heat that had troubled the man. In the words of the traveler, "It was the sand in my shoes."

Frequently, it is the little things in life that make the practice of the Christian faith most difficult. Somehow the great trials of life— moments of crisis, of serious illness, of death and bereavement—have a way of raising us to higher levels and bringing us closer to the only source of spiritual strength, namely, our Savior, Jesus Christ.

But how those smaller trials plague us. How they succeed again and again in causing us to fall and stumble. Those irritations at home, those endless vexations at work, those run-ins with neighbors, those petty quarrels at church—all these are the "sand in our shoes." They wear us down and frequently wear our Christianity thin.

We know that they shouldn't have this effect. It is particularly in coping with these "sand in the shoe" vexations that we cultivate that Christlike love that is patient and kind (1 Corinthians 13:4). It is in the way that we handle these smaller but more persistent irritations that we show our Christian forbearance—or our lack of it.

Where do we get the grace, the spiritual power, to cope with these exasperating vexations? From Christ, who has asked us to "follow Him." He is our great exemplar of patience and kindness. Those who have learned to walk with Christ have learned to take life's hour-by-hour irritations in stride.

Have you been permitting "little things" to get you down? to destroy your happiness? to sour your disposition? to cause you to sin against your loved ones and against your Lord? Ask for pardon in your Savior's name—and ask for a greater measure of His patient, kind love.

Is There a "Marble" in Your Life?

Melissa was frightened. She had put her fist into her mother's expensive vase and was unable to pull it out again.

Unable to help her, Melissa's mother had called the neighbors. Eager to be of help, the man next door had worked with Melissa for nearly 10 minutes, trying to extricate her little fist without sacrificing the jar. Nothing had helped.

Finally he asked Melissa if she could open her fist inside the vase. This would make her hand the same shape it had been in when it slipped into the vase. "Oh, no!" the tearful youngster sobbed. "I'd lose my marble!"

There are many people much older than Melissa who are just as foolish. They want everything that Christianity has to offer—the forgiveness of God, the peace and contentment of faith, the assurance of eternal life—but they don't want to let go of the "marble."

That "marble" may be sinful pride; it may be selfishness; it may be self-righteousness; it may be luxury; it may be the love of money; it may be evil associations; it may be any one of a thousand different things that stand between people and fellowship with God.

The tragic fact is, they don't want to let go of these things! Like Melissa they refuse to open their hand for fear they will lose their precious treasure. In so doing, they jeopardize their soul's salvation.

Is there a "marble" in your life that you should have let go of long ago? Some besetting sin that you have never ceased to coddle? Does it place your spiritual life in jeopardy?

The Bible tells us what to do with every evil that our hands might still clutch: "Let us throw off everything that hinders and the sin that so easily entangles, and let us run ... the race ... . Let us fix our eyes on Jesus, the author and perfecter of our faith" (Hebrews 12:1–2).

Greater Than the Bomb

When a world-famous scientist was asked, "What do you consider your greatest discovery?" he replied, "That I am a sinner and that Christ is my Savior."

In a day of atomic bombs and spaceships, this "greatest discovery" may not seem to be important. Yet it is the greatest discovery that any person can make.

God has given each of us a power that can spell the difference between heaven and hell. This power was made available to us on a little hill outside the city of Jerusalem some 2,000 years ago. There the powers of heaven met the powers of hell, and the powers of hell were vanquished.

When the Son of God, our Savior, died in the place of sinners, the power of Satan was forever broken. The power of God for salvation was let loose on the earth. That is what Paul calls the Gospel of Christ: "The power of God for the salvation of everyone who believes" (Romans 1:16).

Millions of people through the centuries have attested to the power that entered and cleansed and redeemed their lives. Millions of people today can bear witness to that power. Have you made personal contact with the power of Christ's cross? The Bible tells us: "Yet to all who received Him, to those who believed in His name, He gave the right to become children of God" (John 1:12).

In an age of super bombs and super ships, the scientist's personal discovery still remains the greatest: "I am a sinner and Christ is my Savior."

Send for Me!

A young man working in a large factory was spending his first day on a new job. Everything went well until shortly after noon. That's when the machine he was operating began to make an unusual sound.

Eager to demonstrate his mechanical ability, he began to tinker with the machine. Soon it came to a complete stop. Nothing he could do would start the machine again.

Then the foreman walked up. The young man, somewhat embarrassed, tried to explain and defend his actions. He told his superior exactly what he had done, then, shrugging his shoulders, added, "I did my best."

"Young man," the foreman replied, "around here, doing your best means you send for me!"

Our heavenly Father has to remind us often to send for Him. In our foolish pride, we sometimes think that we are doing our best when we apply our puny wisdom to the difficult problems of daily living. We forget that in the vexing trials and temptations of the Christian life, "doing our best" means we send for Him.

"Call on Me" (Psalm 50:15) is still God's command and invitation to His children. "I will deliver you" is still His promise. "And you will glorify Me" is still His holy expectation.

How often each day do we really "send for" our God, who has so graciously promised to help us? "Pray without ceasing," (1 Thessalonians 5:17) the Scriptures admonish us.

Our Lord would have us know we can send for Him at any time. He will help us to do our best.

The Long Look of Lent

While Abraham Lincoln's body lay in state, a great procession of mourners passed by his casket. In the vast throng was an elderly black woman and her 4-year-old grandson. The boy clung to the woman's hand.

As they stood before the bier of the great emancipator, the aged woman stood motionless for a long moment. She looked at the lifeless form of her slain benefactor, tears running down her cheeks.

She stooped and lifted the little boy so he, too, could see the body of the dead president. Wiping the tears from her eyes, the older woman told the boy, "Honey, take a long look at that man. He died for you."

During the Lenten season, Christians pause to take "a long look" at the one who gave His life that everyone might be free. This freedom is not from an earthly taskmaster, but from slavery to sin, death, and the power of the devil.

The Man on the cross who engages our attention during these days is none other than the Son of God. Jesus loved us and gave Himself for us as the Lenten lamb. He bled and died so we might be forever free from the guilt, the power, and the punishment of sin. Christ died for us! He died for our sins (1 Corinthians 15:3).

How important that each of us find time for the long and quiet look of reverent contemplation. Christ deserves more than a passing glance. Ask the Holy Spirit to help you look at Jesus in penitence, with faith, in gratitude, with love, in unconditional surrender.

> Behold the Savior of mankind
> Nailed to the shameful tree!
> How vast the love that Him inclined
> To bleed and die for thee! (*TLH*)

His Face upon Us

It was well past midnight. Richard, who had been asleep in the hotel room for hours, suddenly awoke from a bad dream. Not knowing whether he was alone in the dark room, he whispered in a trembling voice: "Daddy, are you there?"

From across the room came the reassuring voice: "Yes, Richard, Daddy's here." For a minute Richard lay silently, still not quite sure that his bad dream had not been real. Then he whispered, "Daddy, is your face toward me?"

"Yes, my face is toward your bed," the older man replied.

With that assurance the boy closed his eyes and drifted back to sleep. His father was with him, and his father's face was toward his bed.

What a picture of the child of God and the relationship between the heavenly Father and His child! The child of God knows that "the eyes of the LORD are on the righteous and His ears are attentive to their cry" (Psalm 34:15).

Often our lives become so tangled, our minds so weighted with worry and anxiety, our nerves so ragged, that we are almost afraid to face another day. Especially at such moments, we can remind ourselves that God is with us in the darkness and His face is always "toward" us.

As we look into the unknown reaches of the years ahead and our hearts begin to fill with fear, we can find strength and comfort in the immovable assurance that God is already in those years. When we get there, we will find His eyes are still on us.

Because of Christ, God's eyes are the eyes of love, of tenderness, and of deep compassion. Because of what our Savior did for us in Bethlehem, on Calvary's cross, in Joseph's tomb, God has turned His face toward us!

As we daily leave the old behind and step into the new, we can recall the Lord's benediction:

> The LORD bless you and keep you;
> the LORD make His face shine upon you
> and be gracious to you; the LORD turn
> His face toward you and give you peace.
> Amen. (Numbers 6:24–26)

"You Can Tell
He's Been There"

The lecturer had completed his fascinating travelog. One woman said to another, "I always like to hear him describe a country. You can tell that he's been there." She had been impressed by the authority with which the man spoke and by the unimpeachable, firsthand knowledge that lay behind his presentation.

Somehow we feel that the faithful few must have felt the same way about every reference of the Savior to the homeland from which He had come and to which He would return. When He spoke about His "Father's house," He spoke with the authority and the certainty of one who had been there!

No one can read the account of His midnight interview with Nicodemus without being impressed with the clarity, the certainty, and the finality with which He spoke of the things of heaven. "We speak of what we know, and we testify to what we have seen" (John 3:11).

No one could have witnessed that scene in the Upper Room when the Savior spoke fondly of His Father's house without sensing the Savior's intimate and accurate knowledge of the "house" of which He spoke. Remember the absolute assurance with which He spoke? "If it were not so, I would have told you." He knew because He had been there!

As one who stands on a mountaintop looking down into the valley beyond and tells his comrades what he sees, so the Savior tells us about His Father's house and ours. The streets of the eternal city are familiar to Him. The mansions of the Father's house stand clear and bright before His eyes. He knows what lies beyond the valley because He has come from there. That is why He can say with assurance: "If it were not so, I would have told you!"

What a comfort to have as our dearest Friend Him who has already spent endless ages in the eternal Father's house. Jesus knows the way. It was His glorious action on Calvary's cross and at Joseph's garden that opened the way to heaven for us.

Thank God that the eternal Guide who

holds our hands is thoroughly acquainted with the mansions of heaven. Acquainted because before the world's foundation, He was there!

Prayers without Words

George was having difficulty saying his prayers. The 3-year-old had struggled with some of the "big words" in the new prayer his mother was trying to teach him, but somehow the words just weren't suited to his little lips.

After repeated attempts, he decided that he had done his best. Taking a deep breath, he rattled his way through a string of unintelligible sounds, then confidently assured his mother, "Jesus can make a prayer out of that."

We don't know how his mother answered, but there is at least one sense in which George's unexpected remark was right. Jesus can make prayers out of our wordless supplications, and He can answer them before we find the words to say.

In his letter to the Romans, Paul tells us: "In the same way, the Spirit helps us in our weakness. We do not know what we ought to pray for, but the Spirit Himself intercedes for us with groans that words cannot express" (Romans 8:26). God's Holy Spirit knows the inmost wishes of our heart, even those we cannot put into words. He carries those unspoken wishes before the throne of grace.

Sometimes we are prone to judge prayer by the beauty of its prose, by its measured cadences, or even by the eloquence of the person praying. There is nothing wrong in sending our petitions heavenward in our best language. Our God deserves the best we have, even when we pray to Him.

But the language doesn't determine the worthiness of the petition. Instead, the Spirit of God occupies our heart and knows our innermost wants and wishes. He bears those wishes to the throne above "with groans that words cannot express." It is God Himself, through His Holy Spirit, who can take our wordless sobs and give them wings and send them soaring to the heavens. It is He who can "make a prayer" out of our most inarticulate groanings.

> **For He can plead for me with sighings**
> **That are unspeakable to lips like mine;**
> **He bids me pray with earnest cryings,**

Bears witness with my soul
    that I am Thine,
Joint heir with Christ, and thus may
    dare to say:
O heav'nly Father, hear me when I pray!
(*TLH*)

The Oldest Company

It happened at the noonday luncheon of a local business organization. The dishes had been cleared away, and the meeting had been called to order. After the reception of new members and the introduction of visitors, the chairman asked who represented the oldest company in the community.

A young man in the back of the room hesitated for a moment, then said: "I believe I do, sir. I am a minister of the Gospel. The company I represent was founded some 2,000 years ago. I am happy to say that it is still flourishing."

His announcement was greeted with applause. No one was inclined to contradict the man. Everyone agreed that his company was still a going concern.

About 20 centuries ago, the Founder of this company said: "On this rock I will build My church, and the gates of Hades will not overcome it" (Matthew 16:18). And the intervening centuries have proven His startling prediction to be true!

Across the globe, from east to west, from north to south, the company of Christ's redeemed have proclaimed the message of salvation. Millions of people scattered over the face of the globe claim membership in the blessed company of the redeemed.

Elect from ev'ry nation,
Yet one o'er all the earth,
Her charter of salvation:
One Lord, one faith, one birth.
One holy name she blesses,
Partakes one holy food,
And to one hope she presses
With ev'ry grace endued.

It was that "company" that the young minister represented—the oldest, grandest, and largest to be represented at the meeting. It is to that "company" that we belong through faith in Christ, our Savior.

Are you conscious of the glorious fellowship we have by virtue of our membership in the company of Christ? We are "fellow citizens with

God's people and members of God's household, built on the foundation of the apostles and prophets, with Christ Jesus Himself as the chief cornerstone" (Ephesians 2:19–20).

Thank God we belong to His company.

The Word for the Moment

Bishop Taylor was one of the chiefs of chaplains in the English army during World War I. It is said that he applied a simple test to all British clergymen who volunteered to serve as chaplains during that conflict.

Holding his open watch in his hand, the bishop would say to each volunteer: "I am a dying soldier. I have only one minute to live. What must I do to be saved?"

If during the ensuing minute the applicant would say, "Believe in the Lord Jesus Christ, and you will be saved," or words to that effect, he would be accepted. If he gave any other answer, he was rejected.

Whatever else may be said of the bishop's test, surely he knew the only saving message in the moment of death. In that moment, nothing but the divine assurance of full, free, and final forgiveness through Jesus Christ, our Savior, will bring peace to an anxious soul.

No pious platitudes, no honeyed words about a God "in general" who loves the world "in general" and who will take the human race "in general" to some "beautiful isle of somewhere" will bring strength to our step as we walk into the valley of the shadow.

Above all, no attempt to draw comfort from our own past record of achievement will bring light into the gathering darkness of that moment. No one will know better than we that our good words and deeds have been as filthy rags (Isaiah 64:6).

The word for that moment will always and only be: "Believe in the Lord Jesus, and you will be saved" (Acts 16:31).

Believe that God in His mercy sent His Son to be your Savior and that on the altar of the cross, His Son atoned for your entire guilty record. Believe that in Jesus Christ you have a Savior-Shepherd who gave His life for you and has promised to guide you safely through the dark valley of death to the bright mansions of His Father.

Millions who have stood at the door of death and have crossed its threshold will attest that this was "the word for the moment."

Big Brothers or Sisters

It is a familiar sight to see a carefree 2-year-old venturing boldly forth from the safety of home, followed by a "big brother" or "big sister." The older sibling has been sent by a loving parent to see that nothing happens to the little one.

The Bible tells us that our Father's house above is filled with legions of "big brothers." These holy angels have the constant duty of guarding and keeping us. The Scriptures say of this angel throng: "Are not all angels ministering spirits sent to serve those who will inherit salvation?" (Hebrews 1:14). And the Bible also says: "He will command His angels concerning you to guard you in all your ways; they will lift you up in their hands, so that you will not strike your foot against a stone" (Psalm 91:11–12).

Amid grave perils, when dangers threaten within and without, we can be strengthened by the assurance that one of our "big brothers" is walking by our side. After a night of dark and anxious hours, we are able to greet the new morning with the words of Daniel on our lips: "My God sent His angel, and he shut the mouths of the lions. They have not hurt me" (Daniel 6:22).

What comfort for us who are God's children by faith in Christ Jesus to know that our heavenly Father has sent a bigger, stronger brother to stand guard over us and to deliver us from every evil!

We don't need to doubt or fear. We can go about our daily tasks, confident of His loving and divine protection. At the end of the day, when we close our eyes in sleep, we can place our lives into God's keeping with the prayer:

> Lord Jesus, since You love me,
> Now spread Your wings above me
> And shield me from alarm.
> Though Satan would devour me,
> Let angel guards sing o'er me:
> This child of God shall meet no harm.

It Was Only a Poor Mission

It was only a poor mission on a side street in the poorer section of town. Freshly painted and clean, it stood out in striking contrast to the crumbling buildings and disorderly storefronts that surrounded it.

Over its humble entrance, painted in black letters on a white board, was the simple sentence: "We Preach Christ Crucified."

I had, of course, read that sentence a hundred times before. I had heard it in sermons, read it in tracts, seen it on bulletin boards, and had personally used it again and again in conversation.

Somehow this evening the words took on new meaning. As they spoke to me from the crudely painted signboard, they seemed like an echo from the distant past. Nearly 2,000 years ago, the apostle Paul had written those identical words to a mission in the godless city of Corinth.

To the Corinthians, and to all who would read his letter, Paul wrote: "We preach Christ crucified: a stumbling block to Jews and foolishness to Gentiles, but to those whom God has called, both Jews and Greeks, Christ the power of God and the wisdom of God" (1 Corinthians 1:23–24).

With that simple but heaven-sent message, a scattered group of little "missions" was destined to turn the world upside down for Christ. After all the very power of God was in that message (Romans 1:16).

The apostles preached not only Christ, but Christ crucified. Not only Christ the great prophet, the great teacher, the great religious leader, but Christ the Sin-Bearer, the Substitute, the Sin-Atoner, the Mediator, "the Lamb of God who takes away the sin of the world" (John 1:29).

That was the message that, according to the signboard over its entrance, was to be proclaimed to the people who would gather that evening in the mission.

Privileged people! More privileged than thousands who would gather tomorrow in splendid cathedrals from whose pulpits the Gospel of the crucified Christ would not be heard.

It was only a poor mission, but if it remained faithful to the signboard above its door, it could be the gate of heaven for all who entered.

Sunset and Sunrise

I was flying due west, far above the horizon-to-horizon carpeting provided by a layer of fleecy white clouds a thousand feet beneath us.

As the early evening hours wore on, the soft carpet behind us gradually turned into a bluish gray. Its far edges blended silently into the darkness of approaching night. The long stretch of downy carpet that still lay ahead was spectacularly bright. It was splashed with a riot of brilliant color.

In the distance ahead, the blood-red sun was slipping beneath the billowy clouds. It painted the floor beneath the plane first gold, then red, then a deepening purple.

In a few moments, the sun was gone. The carpet of clouds beneath the plane gradually disappeared from view. All was inky darkness. As I leaned back in my seat, I mused on the sermon of the sunset. For every sunset does preach a sermon to the believing heart.

The plane sped on into the night. As I looked out into the gathering darkness, I realized that the miracle I had witnessed had been both a sunset and a sunrise. The same sun that had slipped beneath the far horizon had at the very same moment risen on a new morning in a land beyond my view.

To the hearts that have found eternal life in Jesus Christ, the end of "life's little day" is both a sunset and sunrise that ushers them into the light of God's eternal day.